MANIFESTATION
mastery

MANIFESTATION
mastery

HOW TO SHIFT
YOUR REALITY
& CO-CREATE WITH
THE UNIVERSE

A Channeled Text

CHRISTINA RICE

Published and distributed by Merack Publishing.

Library of Congress Control Number: 2021922182

Manifestation Mastery: How to Shift Your Reality & Co-Create with the Universe
Paperback - 978-1-957048-01-7
eBook - 978-1-957048-02-4
Hardcover - 978-1-957048-03-1
Audiobook - 978-1-957048-04-8

dedication

This is for you—you're ready to experience your own magic.

contents

introduction

What to Know Before You Begin

If you've never read a channeled text before, I'm excited for this to be your first experience. I'll remind you that it is always up to you to discern what resonates and what doesn't—the same way you would with any information. Just because information is channeled does not mean that it must be the objective truth for you—it is just a perspective. That being said, you will feel the difference in frequency between this message and how most people communicate.

The text in this book is a channeled message from an energy called the Monarch Being, offering their perspective on how manifestation and energetic attraction really work so you can consciously shift your reality and live in alignment with your soul's desires. When I channel the Monarch Being, I palpably feel a concentrated stream of divine feminine energy surrounded by a vortex of divine masculine energy, infused with pure love. They describe themselves as being in and of everything, everywhere, all around. When asked about their name, they reference their goal to empower each individual to be the leader for themselves, and to see themselves in all others. My experience with them has been one of love, directness, and expansion.

An important piece of the text is not necessarily the words themselves, but the frequency of the information. Channeling often feels like receiving a packet of information and finding words to convey that which there are no accurate words for. The Monarch Being does not always use proper grammar, and sometimes the words might seem to be oddly chosen or placed. You might notice specific phrases they use regularly, sometimes in ways that don't honor the standard rules of writing. Speaking it out or hearing it spoken might allow you to better grasp what they are communicating.

They are transferring a frequency through the words. These are the "codes" in the words that they refer to. It is not always about the specific words or sentences—it's more about the energy behind them. Every sentence is stated in a specific way for a purpose, whether or not it makes sense to the logical mind. You might notice your energy shifts as you read the text, which is your vibration responding to the codes in the message. It might also feel like you're receiving energy work as you move through the information—notice if you feel tingles or energy flowing in different areas of your body.

When it comes to a channeled text, it's not always about fully absorbing the content of what is said, but simply being in the energy of it. The information will be transferred to you on an energetic level whether or not your logical mind understands everything shared.

You'll also notice that the text is very much a stream of consciousness, not organized the way you might see in other books. They share the information in the order they feel is best, looping back to previous concepts to tie it all together, or if they sense a reminder is needed. I invite you to let yourself go with the flow of the conversation.

If it interests you, I would also encourage you to read the text as many times as you feel called to, because you will get something different out of it every time. You'll find that every sentence has so much depth and multiple meanings that you might not have picked up on before. You can spend as much time with it as you like.

I encourage you to read this text with an open mind and heart, and know that it is not meant to tell you what your truth is—only you can decide that for yourself, as they say (which I agree with). I hope this information expands your mind and your heart the way it did mine, and helps you step into your freedom, truth, and power.

MANIFESTATION
mastery

A CHANNELED TEXT

part one

The Energy of the Intention Itself

We are so excited to be with you here today, dear one, and to start to uncover the truths around manifestation that perhaps have been lost amongst many of you. Our intention for this channeled text transmission is to illuminate for you how you can effortlessly and wonderfully activate miracles in your own lives, improve your own lives in the ways that are for your highest and best, and allow you to see the beauty of your multidimensionality and power that perhaps has been lost or forgotten along the way.

We will warn you that with this information, much of your world will begin to shift, and part of the responsibility of reading this text is to allow yourself to be open to receiving the transmissions, the codes, that are in the words themselves, for there are codes that will unlock what has been forgotten in you for some time—through the words alone. And with this text there is a process of unraveling what you might have known before. Be gentle with yourself, and kind, and also find compassion for others, around those who perhaps have not been able to yet see that the world is not as it might seem to them, but rather there is so much more available to so many of you than you even knew.

What you choose to do with this is up to you, but we encourage you to set your intention now—what is your intention in reading this transmission? Why is it that you wish to unlock your effortless powers of manifestation?

We teach much on what we call foundational frequency, and it is going back to what you perceive to be the "beginning" that allows you to see the roots from which your manifestations grow. We invite you to see manifestation as a natural process for you—you are always doing it, but where your society has glamorized it is to make it seem like it is only what you perceive to be "positive." And through this text, you will realize that what is "positive" and what is "negative" is all in your perception, and you can decide where you wish to relabel, and in doing so, shift your reality. For if you decide that what is positive is actually negative, and what is negative is actually positive, you will see how your entire world shifts upside down, but who is to say that isn't what is right side up anyway?

Your life can be effortless, and to live completely in awareness of your manifestations allows you to create the flow that so many of you seek. We understand that these teachings and this text will bring up much for you in terms of your beliefs around what is and isn't possible, who you are, how things must be, and the first task for you is to realize that all is simply a belief. Even that which you believe to be objective truth— we challenge you to, during this text, for a moment set that aside and simply try on the hat of—it is *all* simply a belief, and from there you can expand your consciousness. Go back to your old beliefs as you so wish—for what we wish to impress upon you more than anything else is—it is all choice.

And through this work you can find yourself to be more empowered and more confident than ever before—for in this information you will face head-on the realization of how much power you have—that you are one with the universe, that you are an extension of it, not separate, and you are working with the cosmic flow of things to experience that which is part of your Soul's path, to experience the lessons it must for its next stage of evolution, and that your Soul's choices are expressed through you—and part of your lesson is to be at peace with this.

We offer a perspective that perhaps you have uncovered and perhaps you have not, but either way, we invite you to be fully open to receiving it. Set your intention—what is it you wish to unlock through this text? And why is it? Honesty is the key to unraveling where you want to go and why you want to go there, and then why you do or why you don't get there, and what ends up happening when you do. It is to go back to the root. Think of your intention, the frequency of your intention, and that is the quality of the deep roots in the soil, and without their vitality your flower cannot grow and bloom. How are you nurturing that intention? Are you remembering that frequency? And this is what we will begin with—it is the energy of the intention itself.

Most of you focus on what is above the surface, but what about what is growing beneath? The more you focus on this (the unseen), the more you will see what is possible manifest in the physical—through this analogy, as the flower that blooms. But where it all began was in a place you could not see, yet this is the most important aspect to consider for longevity and creation. What is it that you are planting? And how are you planting it? How are you taking care of it? Providing sun? Watering? What is the quality of the soil in which you plant? All of this is relevant to what you wish to create coming to fruition. And do you see how if you plant something but do not take care of it, it either will not grow, or as it grows it will not be healthy, and you will not create that which you had dreamt of in the first place?

We invite you to reflect back on this flower again and again, and ask yourself to be honest about the energy of the roots themselves. And this is a key piece of creating something loving, that is the essence of love—the roots must be in love. Remember that you must be rooted in the frequency you wish to create in your reality, to see in your reality, in order for it to grow strong in essence. And you will be tested. When it has not bloomed above the earth, do you trust that the seed is growing, laying strong roots? Or do you question it, get upset, and give up on the watering, the sunlight, the care?

Nurture that which you wish to create in this world, and you will see it come to light. Give it room to breathe, give it room to twist and turn and grow in ways that you might not have expected. It can be greater than you could have ever hoped for, and from this you see how much your "hopes" limit you. Think bigger, dream bigger, and don't be afraid to stand firm in what you know is possible, even if those outside of you make you feel like it cannot be so. When another attempts to remind you of your limitations, have compassion, and simply allow them to be in their limitations if that is where they choose to live.

But you, dear one, are always able to expand—your essence is expansion—do not forget. Part of this testing journey you have been on is to start to remember what you can do, and what a joyous miracle you feel when you fully remember what you are capable of! And from this knowing you release the resentment, the frustration, the resistance that you are so used to as your human self, and instead you allow yourself to break free, to co-create with your human self and with the divine— the support all around you, and this is where you set yourself free. Liberation is all in your mind, if you allow yourself to be in the frequency of it.

part two

How Do You Manifest?

How do you manifest? We remind you that you are always manifesting, so the first step is to ask yourself what you are already calling in. This step of awareness is one that many shy away from, but in fact it is a powerful way for you to realize what is currently being created and how you might wish to shift it. Remember, honesty sets you free, and why so many of you are "unable" to make shifts in your lives is because you are not being honest. You have been so used to the illusions and delusions and hypnosis that you are not even comfortable with truth, a powerful frequency that makes so many of you back away, label as harsh—and this is perhaps one of the biggest misconceptions of all. If you were to perceive the frequency from a neutral state, feel in your body if it expands you or truly feels heavier.

One way you have been trained to stay stuck in your box, to not control your reality, is to have gotten used to what you call "lies," and we call "illusions," as your natural state, as they are all around. And this is where the box begins to break, and you already feel resistance because you refuse to believe that things are so radically different than they might seem, but what if this was the road to your endless, complete, total happiness all along?

We will remind you of this—it is not who you truly are to be filled with sadness, anger, disappointment, grief, and resentment as your natural, consistent state. Simply put, everything that doesn't feel good is not who you really are (if you choose it not to be), but rather a signal of an illusion, within you or around you, an incongruence, or where to make a choice to put you back on your path of highest alignment and truth.

But in truth is where you can see so clearly, and much of your lesson is to get comfortable with truth—hearing it from others, telling others, but above all else, telling yourself. For the purpose of your own growth, and also for those of you wishing to connect with the divine—this is based on the highest truth and love, and being in that frequency is what allows you to be so incredibly open to the information that must come through. Do you trust yourself with the truth? We invite you to ponder this...

How do you manifest? You are always manifesting, we remind you. How do you shift your reality? Remember that you are a co-creator. Remembering that you are a co-creator is the first step. For so many of you believe that the world is against you—you have glorified the underdog becoming the hero through much trial and hardship, and while this can be a rewarding path, we invite you to rework your perception so that you are in full knowing that the universe is fully supporting you, loving you, inviting you to work with it rather than against it. The sign that you are working against it rather than with it *is* the resistance, is feeling stuck in low-frequency emotions—everything that is heavy and burdensome for long periods of time. That deep knowing in your soul that something is off—listen to this! Again we come back to being honest with yourself, for that is the key to all.

And so, make a list of what is being attracted into your life right now—your career, friendships, money, opportunities. What do you like, and what do you not? What do you wish to change? What is the quality of all of these connections? Anywhere that you are not entirely happy, what is it that doesn't make you happy? And then, with honesty, why did you attract this into your life? (We invite you to remember, to attract is not the same as to consciously choose, and is not, as much of your society understands the word, to "deserve." This is a teaching on the energetics of attraction.) What is it teaching you? Where is it a vibrational match for you? What is it bringing up within you? What does it mirror for you? Who does it remind you of? Some of this you might immediately see, and some is yet to be known.

You see, the more you understand how the universe works, you will see that it is a complex, beautiful interweb of cosmic connection, all of the strings tying you all together, so beautifully woven, and in fact, nothing is coincidence. Can you believe this? Nothing is coincidence. And in that knowing you are being called to step into responsibility—this is part of stepping into your power.

part three

Being of the One

How are you the co-creator? It is time for you to remember who you really are, as so many of you think of yourselves as separate from the Universe, God, Source, and some of you don't see that at all. What are your beliefs around how it all works? For some of you, the question feels too big, so you simply set it aside as something to deal with later. But in fact, this is the key that unlocks your desires! You are avoiding the key. You want to open the door, but you don't want to find the key. Now is the time to find it.

We will put it quite simply. Everything is energy, and you are all energy. Where does this energy come from? It is all from the same One, yet you perceive it to move and shift and change. This energy takes different forms, vibrates at different frequencies, and sometimes you can see it with your 3D senses, but often you cannot. Realize that what is in existence is far beyond what you can perceive with your 3D senses. You understand this in air, and in love—but you perceive them as "different things." Understand that they are in fact made up of the same thing—energy, from the same One.

And so as you look around and see everything in your surroundings, your furniture, your body, your emotions, the scents, realize that while it takes different form, it is all of the One, and although you perceive things as all different and separate, the desk and the chair and the empty space between, it is in fact all the One, just at different frequencies. And if you were to shift your perception and see from another dimension, you would simply see oneness, but in your dimension you perceive three things—the desk and the chair and the empty space between. So as you look around, play with the idea that you are simply in the sea, one of many floating in the water, and all together this is the ocean. It is to see the ocean as not just the water but rather the water and the creatures and the sunken ships and everything in between, all in One, together, all from One.

And so, understanding that you are of the One, and in the One, all at once, you can see that you are a manifestation, a form of the One, and thus the One is within you. We remind you that you might see this One as God, Source, the Universe, or however you wish to describe it. Everything around you is a reaction to your frequency, and your frequency is made up of your thoughts, beliefs, emotions, behaviors, and connected energetic beings—we will separate them out into beings for ease within this text. What we mean is how you spend your time, who you spend it with, what you spend it in, all of the people and things you are connected to most directly, as you are all truly connected. This is true of what you perceive in this expression, and the other stored expressions of your Soul that are continuing to be experienced in an alternate manifestation.

And so, as an expression of the One, it is part of your journey to remember that you have power from the One, and it is to work with this rather than against it, and remember that the universe all around you is looking to harmonize—for resonance is what propels you forward, and that which is not resonant will move to what is resonant. The universe is looking for harmony, and when you remember this you can call forward your divine helpers, the other energies of the One, those of a higher dimension and frequency, and ask for support and guidance. And we will also note that, although we represent them as others, they are truly simply other expressions of yourself, which is why you have direct access when you are connected to the same wavelength, so to speak. If you are operating on a lower frequency, you will not be harmonizing with the higher frequencies, which is what so many of you seek.

As you move through your lives, you are always co-creating, with every choice, action, behavior, and thought. Your choice pushes you forward. At the same time that you are co-creating, creating as you go, there is also a sea of possibilities already in existence—infinite possibilities and timelines that in fact already exist, but you are choosing as you go along what you are moving into, and this can shift all the time. There is a working between your Soul's decisions from "outside" this incarnation, and those you are making now—but it is relevant to understand that your Soul, expressed at a higher frequency "before" you took a physical body in your current dimension, as it is more purely expressed at this high frequency, in a sense "overrides" what you might "choose" or attempt to create while incarnated in a physical body. (But you will not perceive it to be so, as separate, or two different paths, if you are in soul alignment and harmony.)

And so, part of your task is to harmonize with your soul, to be at peace with the lessons it chose to learn, and to work with your path, while also taking responsibility for choice and *also* being in creation as you go. If you wish to fully step into your ability to choose what you manifest, it is time to let go of the beliefs that the world is against you, that things must be hard, that resistance is the way, and that life happens to you and you simply see what has been dealt. While this is one way to be, this is not what you are interested in if you are reading this text—you are ready for something so much greater, so much more powerful. You are ready for an extraordinary life.

In fact, this is part of your Soul's mission, to remember how to fully optimize your path, to take control where you can, to drive your own ship, and to break past the limitations of humanness that so many of you feel you are tied to. This is why you feel frustrated even when you don't know what about—because you *know* deep in your soul that you have more abilities, more control, more opportunities. It is the feeling that something is always missing, but you don't know what. That there is more, but you don't know what. That you are on the edge of something, but you do not know what. The time is here, and with this knowing you will unlock the life that you are truly meant to live—with full clarity, full honesty, and full love for yourself and your past. For as you see more of yourself, and more of how you are of the One, you step into deeper and deeper love for yourself and for others, and this is magnetic for you. In being love, you attract more love, and so we begin.

part four

How to Become an Effortless Manifestor

We will start to break down for you the process of manifestation, but we remind you to begin with what you have already manifested into your life, in what you perceive to be the past, and in the now, so you can start to really understand what your frequency is putting out and what you are attracting in. If you do not like what is in your reality, this is a sign that you are not truly in alignment with who you are, and the more you understand who you are and send that signal to the universe, you will see your reality shift.

And so, understand that as we use the term "manifestation" from here on out, we are going to assume it is what you want (in the sense of what feels joyful and expansive for you), rather than what you don't want, unless we specifically say otherwise, for ease of communicating in this transmission.

How is it that you manifest what you *do* want? It is so much simpler than you think, yet also so much more complex, for we must take into account all of the ways you are sending messages to the universe, what you are sending out, and also the free will of others around you and what they are sending out as well. We will remind you that what you can control, and how you can choose, is for yourself, and this creates a ripple effect around you. Anywhere you are waiting on someone else to shift your reality, or worried about their choices or actions, is where you are releasing your own power and forgetting who you really are. It is not about any other—this is about you, of the One, and your life. When you are spending energy and attention focusing on another, this is taking away from what you can be magnetizing for yourself, and also filling you with a frequency typically that is not conducive to what you wish to attract. And, as you will later come to uncover, it is focusing on your own frequency, signaling, and choice that is the truest, most powerful way to support others, in the end.

Overall, we will invite you to look at these steps:

- Set a clear intention.
- Ask.
- Follow the guidance.
- Do not settle for less, unless you want that.
- Remember that you already have it.
- Celebrate that you already have it.
- Act on the frequency.

It is simple—be the frequency you want to attract. In being, you are, and what you are, is what you have, and more of your being is magnetized to you.

What is it to be an effortless manifestor? When you do the deeper root-cause work, the process becomes simple, and this is what we wish to speak more on. So many of you believe that manifesting is a one by one process, but when you focus on your own alignment, the manifestation is a natural side effect, because you are who you truly are. So many of you are focusing on what is in fact actually less important, and in doing so, you make the manifestation process more difficult.

What is it to become an effortless manifestor? Raise your vibration. And this is shifting your thoughts and beliefs. It is in optimizing your physical vessel and paying attention to all that brings you down—more than you might think. It is releasing the relationships that are pulling you down. Clearing out low-frequency emotions.

Many of you think of raising as pushing upwards, but it is not to push upwards, but to think of yourself as a balloon weighed down by a number of strings attached to weights on the earth. As you cut the strings that pull you down, you naturally float up higher and higher. You can also see this as something blocking your expansion in every direction—as something that has put you in a box that you are so much greater than, and if you allow the walls to fall down, you can see what is so much greater around you and allow yourself to expand into that. And we ask you, when you think of being tied down by the strings on the balloon, what comes to mind for you? What people, responsibilities, and emotions are weighing you down? The deep work is to allow those strings to be cut lovingly and to allow yourself to be set free.

When releasing what is holding you down, there is much that blocks many of you—the strong power of your mind! When your mind starts chattering, realize that it is replaying whatever programming has been ingrained. This is where you can start to separate the programs playing from what is in alignment with your soul's truth, which will always feel resonant. Think of it as simply changing the song on the radio. If you've been listening to the same song for years, you can choose another that feels happier and more uplifting. When your mind starts chattering, you can listen to it with love. There is no need to get upset or react, your mind is simply replaying what it has been programmed to play, and this is in fact a helpful space to uncover where the programming was learned. This is where, from an energy of honesty, you can ask your mind where it learned this lesson, and go back to the beginning. Why was it taught that? Who was that for? Does it serve you, or not? Is it truly your own? If it is holding you back from happiness, love, expansion, and purpose, it is not your own—for you *are* happiness, love, expansion, and purpose.

As you uncover where it is from, ask yourself if this programming party, as we will call it, is still in your life. Is it someone you listen to? Someone in your life? From there, you can ask yourself what other programs or beliefs were picked up from that place, and this is how you start to become aware of the programs. When you realize they are *programs* and not truths, you are able to release the programs that you no longer want, and replace them with new truths. Allow yourself to be on this journey, for uncovering all of your programs can take time, and we invite you to approach the process with curiosity and love, an energy of exploration, and not judgment. For when you are in judgment, this is not the frequency you want to be filled with!

When you learn about your programs, approach yourself like you would a young child who had been living with a misunderstanding leading them into worry or unhappiness. For example, if a child never played because they thought they weren't allowed to, and you illuminated for them that they are, in fact, meant to play, you would relay that message with excitement and love, not judgment for their original misconception. What was programmed informed their reality, and how beautiful to be able to open up more possibilities for them! And isn't that a beautiful thing, how simply swapping out older programs can open the door to an entirely new life—from one where you believe you must sit and watch alone instead of play and dance and laugh as you want... as you are meant to.

It is shifting what seems like the simplest beliefs that can create a whole new world for you. Sometimes these beliefs are so simple that they are overlooked, but this is where we will remind you to set the intention that you are open to *all* old programs coming to light, and nothing is too unimportant to be in awareness of. This is a spring cleaning of your beliefs, what is filling your brain, and this requires care, love, and time. It is an exploration, and with every bit of the journey, you feel more and more lightness enter your life. *Enjoy* the journey. Enjoy the exploration, and more and more will come your way.

We know that one of the most common forms of resistance you cling to is the belief that you cannot. But realize where you have been misusing this term—this is another play of responsibility. You *choose* not to—everything is a choice. Your brain might have decided there are only two choices, or even one, to keep things simple, for if your brain were to evaluate the infinite possibilities always available to you at every moment, it might explode, and so it protects itself and tries to deduce all of the possibilities into the least amount for ease of moving through the world.

However, what affects this filter? Why is it that your brain chooses to see the two that feel low frequency rather than the two most expansive choices available to you, amongst the infinite? The more you clean out your programs, the more you will see how this filtering naturally shifts, and the more expansive choices are presented to you. The choices your brain focuses on are a reflection of the programs it has been running, and so as you swap out what you believe to be the rules of your brain, your brain sees new choices. Think of it as reprogramming your video game—there is a new set of rules and instructions—and now you are in awareness of your choice, rather than being unconscious of it all.

When your belief that you cannot or there is only one way comes up, take a moment to reflect and open up your energy body to any other options. This is where you can allow your creativity to come out—for the more you are in creativity, the more you are able to see more choices—they naturally drop in! It is accessing different energies you already have that allows you to see more, and where you have only been driving down one road your whole life, you will start to see the infinite tangents from that road and the many places you can go, if you so choose.

And what of your family? Of your boss? Your coworkers? The friends from youth that won't seem to leave you alone? It is time to be honest with yourself about the relationships in your life. One of the most powerful exercises you can do to reset your energy body is to take time alone for yourself to be in your own energy—a good amount of time, such as a week— where you are purely by yourself, without any other potential programs or energies getting in your way, and then as you re-enter what was your "normal" life, start to notice the shifts in how you feel, where there is worry, resentment, intensity, and so on.

And as you do this work you will start to notice more and more what is not in alignment, what you do not enjoy, and we will remind you that joy and happiness and love are who you are. This is your truth, and so the question is not—*do I deserve it?* Because of course you "deserve" what you already are, in your truth. Does a rose deserve to be a beautiful rose? Of course, because it is a rose! And it is for the happiness of all that it is the purest, highest expression of itself. And so you are the same. It is your birthright, your mission, your duty, if you are in alignment with serving *all*, the One, and yourself, which are all one, to be the purest, highest expression of yourself.

With that, it is to notice where others might be affecting you so that you are not showing up fully as that highest, purest expression of yourself. It is not for your or their highest and best when you are in a relationship that you do not feel you are your highest expression in, for the energetic connection between you is not of the highest frequency, and this affects you both.

Envision the energetic cord between you as a specific color. Your favorite color is the color of the bond that you are meant to have—you are connected with love. Your least favorite color is what drags you down—and if that energetic connection is your least favorite color, it is tying both of you to an energy that is bringing both of you "down," so to speak. Remember that everything you are connected to will affect your frequency— these are all cords that will play a part in how you feel, and so looking into relationships is a crucial part of the process to take conscious control of your manifestation process.

What is it that you are truly afraid of? For most of you, it is that another will not come, but the truth is that if releasing allows you to be in a higher frequency, then you will also attract in that higher frequency, and so by the laws of the universe what you perceive to be "better" will of course come.

part five

On the Topic of Family and Coworkers

You might stop yourself because you feel that you must stay attached to family—for what if there is a member of your family who is pulling down your vibration, making you feel small, not enough, not worthy, not lovable, and so on? Well, this is a helpful point for you to grow, to see within them things about yourself, in terms of what is reflected back to you and how this is an opportunity to cement in and expand your strength, but we will also remind you that to stay attached to your "family" is also a choice that you have the right to make, but it is to take responsibility for that choice.

If your family is "dragging you down," so to speak, and you are in ownership of staying in that relationship despite how it might be affecting you, that alone will help to raise the vibration, and because your intention is strong and pure and from a place of love, now the energetic attachment is not pulling you down in the same way. What is important, we will remind you again, is the frequency of your decision—the roots. What is it based on? Where is it coming from? Is it coming from a place of true love, or a place of resentment and obligation? If, however, you are in full realization that the relationship is not serving you in your highest, is not supporting you in your expansion and truth, and you do not wish to make the decision to stay in the relationship, where do you judge yourself? And why do you judge yourself? When you are caught up in the expectations of others, this is where you lose sight of who you really are, and the infinite possibilities that can exist.

In all aspects, when evaluating how things are affecting your frequency, ask yourself, *Is this supporting my expansion? Is this supporting me in feeling and being the way I wish to feel and be?* To answer honestly will be a simple way to discern what is lowering your vibration and what is not. What blocks so many of you are your beliefs about family and why you must stay together. Understand the evolutionary roots, for you do not want to be forgotten by the "tribe," but as your world has changed, you are able to see beyond the way your brain is programmed, and that is part of your expansion. If you were to live your life based on primitive instincts, there would be many things that would go awry in your life, for you see how things open up when you notice what is your primitive brain compared to what is your soul speaking, and through this text we are teaching you to listen to your soul.

The idea of family has become distorted, and the program that has been run is that family always stays with each other and you love your family no matter what, but the deeper question is—is family only based on blood? And what is that concept of love? For this is one place where your society has completely misunderstood the idea of love, which is not from obligation. Obligation and dedication are not the same as love, although they might overlap. It is key not to confuse the three.

And who is to gain when you are living with the belief that you must put the happiness of others above your own? This is where you are feeding into the hierarchy, and acting from a misunderstanding of how energy around you works. Where you keep yourself in a lower state of consciousness is when you believe it is this *or* that, that someone's happiness must be put above another, and here we find lack mindset, which we will speak more on throughout this transmission, but it is time to move beyond this. For when you are acting in the highest for yourself, you are acting in the highest for all around you, because you are all of the One. In staying in a low-frequency relationship, neither party is able to fully expand into their greatness, for that low-frequency energy cord is pulling both down, and then what lessons are both of you missing out on because you are staying stagnant?

Do not feed another with an energetic cord of anger, resentment, sadness, obligation, or insecurity. Feed only with love. Give and receive love, the purest love, a love you might not have even experienced before (but you are feeling it, and more on this to come), and you will start to see that giving and receiving love in many ways is one and the same. And so, we invite you to redefine family for yourselves, and take out what you have been told you "must" do. Whenever told what you "must" do—is the intention to control you? This is not an energy you are meant to feed into, because it is time for you to fully step into your natural state of flow, happiness, and love, and time to release any energies that might be leading you astray. The more you become a master manifestor, you will see that as you stay on your highest path of alignment, this serves all around you, and that your clearest compass is to ask what is feeding your soul so purely, and all else aligns beautifully.

And on the topic of coworkers and bosses, as many of you feel stuck in your situation, how can you leave, you ask? *What if this is the way to sustain myself financially?* This is based on a limited mindset of where your money is coming from, how it comes through, and again, where you can notice that your brain is tuning into limited "choices" based on the programs that you have been believing—it is time to expand your mindset! Money comes in many ways, and again, where you stay in an unhappy situation is often rooted in feeling unworthy of something better. But when you tune into your greatest truth that you are of course always worthy of happiness and love, as you are happiness and love, you can see that where there is not happiness is where it is not the right match. And when you are living from that *knowing* (we will say knowing rather than belief), that you are of course love and that you always attract love, when you let go of what is not allowing you to expand, you can experience the opportunities that will.

And sometimes this is a process, but the speed at which it comes to fruition will be a reflection of your rooted knowingness, what is in highest alignment, and how quickly you follow the signals to get there. Another aspect of this process is to notice where you are not seeing the opportunity for growth, because from a higher perspective every opportunity that feels lower frequency can in fact be transmuted, if you so choose. And this is a powerful technique that we invite you to use in many aspects of raising your frequency by releasing what is pulling down your vibration. There is an option to let go, and there is also an option to transmute.

In relation to others who have free will, there might not always be full cooperation or an aligned response, and then you know that the next step is to release when you have transmuted everything you can. But the trick we wish to cover is to see every single connection and interaction as potential for love and happiness, once transmuted. This is the gift you have—to transmute.

What we mean by this is, for example, let's say you are in a job situation with a coworker who is not very nice to you, and every day you go into work feeling depressed and insecure or angry and bitter—now, of course you know this is no way to be! So what we will remind you of is to *anchor* yourself into who you truly are—love and abundance—and carry that into the situation, for you are so powerful, and often you forget your ability to shift energies and to see the bigger picture. As you go into work, and you shift your own energy and the relationship, notice how this creates a ripple effect to the coworker.

As you go into work, remember that it is not about the coworker patronizing or antagonizing you—for this is where you are in the energy of "victimization," as you say—but that every single thing in your path is a reflection of you, which includes opportunities for you to cement in a higher frequency, to overcome challenges that allow for your expansion, and in fact, it is the challenges that allow for your growth the most. The meeting of your vibrations serves you both in one way or another, although it might not be as you expect, but when you are firmly rooted in your frequency you have the chance to transmute, to anchor in more deeply, and to see more truths within yourself. Transformation is always happening.

Think of the lower frequency that could potentially pull you down as the arrow in the bow, pulled back, and then you are able to launch forward. But these "tests," as some of you call them, are chances for you to learn, grow, and stand firm in who you really are. What we will also remind you of is that while you might call them "tests," and we see no issue with using words or terms that allow you to understand concepts easily, we want you to also know that the "test" is not from an energy that you might associate with tests as you know them—it is not a test of worthiness or from the intention to see if you are "good enough," for of course you are good enough. This is energy coming into your field in the form of opportunities, emotions, people, and situations that will either be attracted or reflected based on the energy you radiate out, in combination with choice, and this is how all of the energies of the universe shift around, bobbing through like creatures in the sea.

To be a high-frequency being does not mean that you will never encounter lower frequencies—but do you hold onto them? How do you respond? How do they affect you? You can allow the lower frequencies to quite literally leech onto you or you can allow them to bounce off or float right on by—this is up to you. The lesson in all of this is to remind you that there are *not* only two choices in your situations that aren't serving you, and these are beautiful opportunities for you to *be* the person you truly are—confident, loving, abundant, powerful, and magical beyond belief. For you *are* a master manifestor. You are remembering.

part six

Romantic Partnerships & Neutrality

You can think similarly when it comes to romantic partnerships, and we have a bit more to add on this topic, too. For many of you have misunderstood what the term "love" means, what it is to be in a loving partnership, and we plan on offering another transmission all about this topic and how to discern the difference between true love—its truest frequency—and other frequencies and partnerships. Again, it is not to say one is wrong or right, but to simply be in awareness of what frequency you are aligning yourself with. You are meant to feel safe, heard, and aligned with your truth as love.

When it comes to your romantic partnerships, notice what this person brings out in you, or rather, helps you bring out in yourself, and be open to what you are able to learn about yourself from the reflection that you wouldn't be able to notice before, for there is much growth that can occur in these romantic partnerships. We will also offer to you, again, another program—that is how long a relationship should last, and what it means when a relationship ends "early" or "late," and to realize these terms are arbitrary, and simply labels that you have decided, or have been thrust upon you by society, so now is your time to rewrite the story. And you can, if you so choose, decide that every relationship lasts exactly as it is meant to, and for one to end is not a failure. For if you finish a book, you read the final chapter, and you reach the end, is this a failure because it is over? No, in fact, it is a vast accomplishment!

The duration of every relationship is exactly as it should be, and you will open yourself up to many more opportunities to experience deeper, truer love in all types of relationships if you release judgments or expectations about how long they should last and what it means when they are complete. What a beautiful chapter to have completed, and just as when you finish a book, does this mean it was all for nothing? No, in fact you have learned so much more, and isn't it interesting how you celebrate finishing more books but you judge when relationships end? However, is it to be admired if you read more and more books but don't fully take anything from them? No, for this is not truly expanding you—you weren't allowing yourself to fully be in the process to learn, to grow, to shift through the knowledge inside. It is the same in relationships, and the key is to show up fully and be completely present in the experiences that are offered to you in relationships, so you can fully embrace the learning points while you are there.

You are presented with relationships that will teach you lessons for your highest and best for you to eventually create more things that you have your intention set on, even if you don't see it in the moment. And if these lessons are necessary stepping stones for you to shift your vibration to be in alignment with reaching your goals, then a way to quicken the process to achieving them is to allow yourself to fully be in the lesson in the now, otherwise it will return again in another form. And sometimes these lessons feel like hardship, but it is an opportunity for you to expand out and see how much this obstacle is allowing you to shift, to know, to feel more deeply in a way that will align you with your larger manifestation.

And this is where many of you miss the boat—you set your intention, and you are looking for something in your environment to confirm you are closer, and you judge what pops up next thinking that you know if this is "closer" or not, when in actuality of course it is your next step! But the way you perceive it is based on a limited view from the past, and these opportunities are calling forth the greater aspects of you, for you to align with what you wish to manifest. Be careful not to judge your situations, and if you catch yourself, ask yourself where the judgment is coming from—an old frequency, an old program, an old way of being? Or the version of you that is fully aligned with that which you are calling in? The truth is that if you were already fully anchored into the frequency, it would be in your physical reality already, and so for it to be pulled into your physical reality in the now, you will be presented with opportunities to anchor in this new way of being. When you respond as the you that is not a vibrational match for that which you want, the manifestation does not come through in the physical. We hope you see how these tips can allow you to manifest more quickly and effortlessly.

Many of you might perceive this as seeing things optimistically, with the glass half full always, and yes, you can see it as this, but where many might misunderstand is in feeling like they must always be happy about or optimistic about everything presented, but where you are trying to force this is not really a vibration of truth, and you cannot pretend to be a different vibration. You cannot "trick" the universe—all there is is energy and this is what it responds to. You do not, in fact, need to be positive all the time in order to effortlessly manifest. In fact, you won't feel positive all the time if you feel your full range of emotions. Rather, the "positivity" is often a natural byproduct of unraveling everything that lowers your frequency, because you will rise to your natural state, and you will be so energetically resilient that the lower frequencies won't have the same effect on you as they perhaps once did. We will speak more on energetic resilience in a moment.

The reason we bring up the myth of positivity is because we caution you against suppressing emotions, as this is how they fester in the body. When you do not allow yourself to feel and express your emotions, you miss the opportunity to transmute them, and building this muscle is one of the greatest skills to ever master. We will tell you more about how you can use high-frequency emotions to catapult your manifestation process, but to become master manifestors, as we discuss some of the overall shifts to make, we do not want you to put a blanket of fake positivity on top of everything you are feeling! So as you begin to work through this process, allow yourself to feel all of the emotions, and allow them to come up as needed. We will remind you, the key is to release yourself of all judgment, and that includes judgment of certain emotions.

As you know that certain things make you feel "good" and certain things make you feel "bad," it is not that those things are inherently good or bad, but rather that that is your vibrational response to its energy, and so you can choose to add more of it or take away some of it so that you are in alignment.

We bring this up because an important message for us to share is that for you to continue to unlock your manifestation abilities, you will start to see the power of neutrality as a starting point, and in some ways you can say this is helping you see "objectively," although we think this word is misused quite often as well—what really is objective? But rather it is the lesson of not adding emotionally charged labels to things— what if everything just is? Happiness just is, sadness just is, and sadness isn't inherently bad, for all energy is valuable, all energy is important, and how can that sadness allow you to experience your humanness in a deeper way? How can it allow you to grow and feel and love more deeply? The lesson is to see the value in it all, but where you block yourself is when you label anger, sadness, bitterness as "bad" and so you don't allow yourself to feel them, but this leads to misalignment in your system, for this energy becomes trapped in your body or your consciousness in ways you might not realize, and this can be energy from a long time ago.

Imagine a piece of food that accidentally gets thrown under the bed and is forgotten about, and over time the room starts smelling, and you don't know why, and eventually you find the piece of food, moldy, with bugs around it, and when you finally clean the room things become more pleasant for you again. This is similar to what happens when you leave lower frequency emotions stored in the body. When emotions are held in the body, they are "fed" by other similar frequencies. So if you have anger from childhood stored in your body, as you feel that frequency as an adult and don't allow yourself to transmute it, imagine that emotion getting trapped again, and it sticks to the original "anger"—you can imagine it as an entity within your system, and this amplifies that frequency in your body, and this is how you can feel energies like anxiety and depression and anger in the *now* even though it feels like a mismatch, you don't know why you feel it. This is the importance of an energetic cleanup—allowing yourself to feel the emotions, love on them, without judgment, and let them move through. This is key for manifesting what you want, because this is an unseen reason why many of you might be attracting more of that frequency into your life.

Similarly, if you want more love and happiness, you will want to amplify that energy in your body. Allow the frequency of "joy" to "stick" to the joy in your body, growing and growing, and notice how it feels. And so, you are a master manifestor no matter what, for you are always drawing to you that which you are. But the question is—what is the frequency of what you want to attract in? If you desire to manifest more sadness and drama, you know what to keep in your body. If you want to manifest love and joy, you know what to keep in your body. It is up to you. Remember, this work brings you into the realization of how powerful you already are, and reminds you of your role in creation. The fastest way to make shifts in your life is to end any abdication of responsibility. Everything is working with you. Everything is supporting you, but it will support you in the way that you are telling it to. The language of the universe is energy. What are you saying to it? If you are vibrating with low-frequency energy, the universe will support you in it. If you vibrate with high-frequency energy, the universe will support you in it. It is time for you to clearly convey how you wish to be supported. Yes, dear one, you are *that* powerful.

part seven

Energetic Resilience

Now we will touch a bit more on energetic resilience, for this is an important muscle to build as you master these techniques and co-create with precision and joy. To put it simply, a sign of energetic resilience is to dip yourself into low-frequency energies yet not be affected by them. A good way to test your level of energetic resilience is to spend time around people or in an area that is palpably at a lower frequency than you, on a "different wavelength," quite literally. After spending time there, how do you feel? Do you feel stuck in those low-frequency energies? Do you carry lower emotions from it for a long period of time? Or do you rise back to your high-frequency self, feeling good again?

You will notice as you anchor in a higher frequency that your energetic resilience shifts in stages. Before doing this work, you might feel that after spending time around low-frequency people, you feel like you are sad, angry, pessimistic, or bitter for some time afterward. After some time of working on your vibration, however, you might notice that if you spend time with low-frequency people, you feel a bit off for a little while after, but you're able to shake it off after some time. And then, as you build even more energetic resilience, you'll notice that spending time with low-frequency people doesn't affect your vibration at all, and you are able to hold the frequency! We know many of you struggle with holding your frequency, but realize that this is a muscle to build, and the more you practice, the better and better you get.

How do you build energetic resilience? First, we remind you that it is a process. The first step is to get yourself in a higher frequency, and spending more time alone and with palpably high-vibrational people will help you get into this higher state. Once you are there, you want to spend time there and get comfortable there, so that it becomes your new set point. After some time there, once it is your new set point, you will dip your toes into being around low-frequency energies, and see how quickly you snap back to your new set point. Start small, and over time the muscle will build.

You might notice that at first you require a set ritual or routine to clear yourself, move the energy through, release what isn't yours, and reset your programs, but over time you will not require this, as you are holding the vibration so strongly that nothing is affecting you at all and the lower frequencies are simply bouncing off of you, are passing right by, because there is nothing they can "stick" to within your energetic field. And so you will feel your energetic resilience, and at this point we invite you to notice all of the wonderful things you are drawing into your life.

When we speak about building up your energetic resilience, we are not suggesting you *need* to spend time in lower frequencies, for you most likely will not because you will not feel the vibrational resonance, but it is in building up that muscle so that you are not affected in the way you used to be. You can think of this similarly to the way you understand allowing the body to fully heal, to rest and repair, and then build up, so that it can go out into the world as it once did and not feel sick or tired or weak anymore. It is the same with your frequency, and building your energetic resilience will strengthen the boundaries and force of your energetic field to amplify your magnetism beyond what you could ever believe.

part eight

Amplifying Your Signal

The more you come into the truth of who you are, the more your signal is amplified. This is all in aligning with your soul, your truest self, and everything the truest version of you could desire will come straight to you. For many, you have forgotten yourselves, and much of this is in the busy-ness forced upon you, the "standard" approaches to life that you step into, what you are modeled—you follow the path set out before you, but what about all of the exploration that occurs when you go off-path?

A key piece of becoming a powerful magnet for what you desire is getting to know yourself and what you call living in alignment. What, exactly, does this mean? Well, it is common to live under the illusion that life should feel difficult and forced. This is where we get into the idea of resistance and living in a perpetual state of resistance, which is an energy of forcing, pushing, working very hard and feeling like you're not getting anywhere—where life feels like you are pushing a boulder up a hill, or trying to run with weights tied to your ankles. This, dear one, is not who you are meant to be! Your life can be floating down the riverbank effortlessly, landing exactly where you're meant to go. The choice is yours.

We will go with the assumption that you wish to live floating down the riverbank, and a helpful place to start is to make a list of all the places where you feel unhappy, exhausted, or like you're forcing or pushing. What in your life feels like forcing a square peg into a round hole, as you say? And next to each, how would you like to feel? You know there is another way. And now you are ready to open up your consciousness to how it could be in flow. Sometimes this is a swapping out of physical things, sometimes this is a shift in your energy or perception, but it is to find the switch that brings things to flow.

For example, as you put a puzzle together, sometimes you're trying to put the wrong piece in, but sometimes you simply have to rotate the piece and it fits in perfectly, and this is what it is to explore the shifts to feel things simply snap into place. It is time for smooth sailing! Notice also where in your life things feel easy, effortless, and where you are in that state of flow. What do you genuinely enjoy doing? What feels effortless? What brings you joy? Think of hobbies, activities, and places that allow you to feel peace and joy. What are you naturally good at? For so many of you have been stuck in the business of trying to make another's skills or strengths or enjoyments your own, and this is where you are not in alignment with the unique expression of your soul!

You search for happiness by making another's strengths or skills or enjoyments your own, but even if you master these, you will not feel what you seek to feel because they are not in alignment with your unique expression, and so the faster way to get there is to release what is another's enjoyment or strength and simply focus on how *you* feel and what you are naturally good at. And this is how the universe works together beautifully, how your world was beautifully designed perfectly to all work together if you would simply allow it, if all were to allow themselves to fall into what they were naturally good at and desired to do.

We will remind you that not all others excel at what you naturally excel at, that not all others enjoy doing what you enjoy doing, for a beautiful purpose—for the whole puzzle to fit together! If you feel like you do not know where to begin, what a beautiful journey to learn about yourself again—like meeting a lover for the first time and allowing yourself to explore every piece of them—do this for yourself. Approach life with a childlike curiosity—everything you try gives you new information. Notice what you enjoy and what you do not, what you are naturally good at and what you are not. Gain bits and pieces from every experience, and we caution you against labeling things as all one thing, for there are perhaps high and low-frequency aspects of many experiences, and there is no need to group them all into one. It is here where you can tune into the subtleties of the experience and get to know what you like and what you do not, and enjoy the process of exploration.

This process of uncovering yourself charges your manifestation practice, as you might call it, in a few ways. On one level, it is allowing you to see where you can be in flow, and what you like, so that you can spend more time in these energies rather than forcing or pulling. And second, because it is allowing you to be in the energy of exploration, curiosity, and excitement, and it is here that you can easily receive intuitive guidance from your Higher Self—divine guidance that is of the highest frequency, and also those emotions will put you into the higher frequency that allows you to attract more of what you are curious and excited about, and you see how it all builds from here.

What a fun task to have—to explore yourself and the likes and the dislikes, and through this process you will learn to appreciate what makes you unique, what you are naturally good at that others might not have an interest in, where you feel in your purest state of zen and happiness. Where is it that you lose time? Where is it that you feel totally at peace even if you are in awareness of things that are crazy or busy or "too much" outside of you? This is your key—your key to unlocking peacefulness, stillness, and happiness in your daily life. Think of these as tools in your toolbelt—the things that make you happy. Perhaps it is painting or singing or dancing, playing, rolling on the grass, being by the water, creation in any form... And we will also offer that the more you are in the energy of *creation* in your daily life—creating, creating, creating—that energy is going to amplify the creation within your own life. And so you see, once again, the frequency attracts more of it, and if you wish to master creation, you can be a creator consciously in your life, and apply these principles to how you create your life.

We will use an example of creation in a form you more easily understand, for you to better integrate what it means to be a creator—think about creating a song or a piece of artwork. We will use the example of writing a song. Think about what goes into making a beautiful song—the music, the lyrics, in whatever combinations, and how it is made up of frequencies. And the frequencies are in alignment with the intention, which has already been set beforehand. And for most, with musical creation, it is a reflection of the energy that they feel within themselves, creating music that reflects emotions they feel or have felt at any time, and this energy shifts form and is expressed through music, and so we see the music is a reflection of the energy itself. And so, from intention, inspiration flows. And the creator allows divine inspiration to drop in, whether or not it is labeled as such, and they come up with lyrics and storytelling within the music from that place of creativity, from the place of inspiration, and through the process they are playing and curious and explorative. It is the same as how you create your own life.

And how a message is received by the audience is based on if there is a vibrational match. But also, what about songs that are embedded with love and happiness, the newness of a relationship perhaps, as an example, but it doesn't resonate with the listener? There is power of amplification of a frequency based on how it was charged, and so the purer and clearer the intention, the frequency from which the song was created, the more that energy will be supercharged, and these are in the songs where you *feel* the vibration in your body, where they move you so deeply, because that song was charged with such a pure, powerful, authentic intention, and the frequency is so amplified.

This parallels your power of creation in your own life—and do you see how you can supercharge your energy? Like the song, you start with intention, and you come from clarity with the frequency from which you are building—you are clear on the frequency that you are emitting and sending out into the universe. From there, you allow the divine inspiration to help guide you, for it to take its form and to create what is beautiful, and in doing so, those who are resonant will be magnetized to the song that is your life, and more powerfully so the clearer your frequency is.

But the key with a "hit" song is the excitement and authenticity behind it—what was the energy from which it was written, created, produced? And now you see how this all comes together for you. You can see the parallels between how you create anything that feels a bit more tangible and your life, and the "video game," perhaps, you are creating in every moment—the movable picture that you are painting, designing, imagining in every moment based on what you are wishing to create. And perhaps it starts off with one clear vision, but by the end it is different than what is expected, but you let the frequency guide the way, and it ends up becoming so much better than even your original idea or direction.

And to return to the idea of sending a clear signal to the universe—this is a clear signal of who you are, of what you are, and where you feel that you are a weak magnet, so to speak, is where your signal is clouded and dull, where your vibration is muddled. And the more you untangle what is you and what is not, the clearer you shine, and the brighter you shine, the more what is meant for you can come straight to you—for it can see you, and there is not so much resistance in the way. And so, uncovering what you truly enjoy and what you do not, what your strengths are, your skills, what your own beliefs are, is the key. And as you evaluate your programs, you can decide what are your beliefs and what are not, and we empower you to know that you get to decide what they are—this your choice, your right, and no logic or concrete detail is in fact needed to have certain beliefs—which we are sure you can see based on the many seemingly contradictory beliefs that so many hold.

But the more you peel back these programs, you will realize what is congruent and what is not within your system, with each other, but also with your frequency. For example, to know you are a being of love but to have a belief that you are not worthy of love is incongruent, and what if that incongruence is in fact the source of the discomfort within you rather than an actual belief that you are unworthy of love? This is a thought, another possibility you could say, to allow you to see that perhaps they were not your own beliefs at all, which is why your body signals to you it is uncomfortable, and then you can decide to release what isn't a match. In every moment, you can decide how to see what is in front of you, and what frequency you wish to embody.

In emitting a clear signal—the clearest form of your energy, the universe sees you, and you manifest more quickly and more powerfully. It is to be firm in who you are, and not who another is, and this is one way that all of the standards, expectations, and step-by-step processes that have been instituted in your society have pulled you away from exploring your uniqueness, but it is that uniqueness that allows you to so effortlessly attract what is uniquely for you. And so we ask, how can you allow your uniqueness to shine through again? What is it that makes you *you*—and the more you broadcast this to the world, the more you will see how your reality shifts.

What pieces of yourself are you afraid to show? Where are you hiding? Where are you hiding from others, and where are you hiding from yourself? What are the pieces you're afraid to explore? Is it worth it to stay a copy of someone else, or to fit in with the status quo, if it means your energetic signal is dull? It is time to shine your light fully, and to release everything that is dulling you from being seen. Where does the fear of being fully seen come from? Why is it that you're afraid to show your true energy? Why is it vulnerable to be seen so clearly? This is where you fear truth—of what is a vibrational match and what is not. But it is time to fully decide—do you wish to live in fear of what you might release, or do you wish to live in the empowerment of powerfully and effortlessly magnetizing greater things than you could have ever imagined? What have your actions aligned with thus far? It is going into the depths of yourself and showing the world your true thoughts, beliefs, emotions, and gifts that will set you free, and you will shine as the bright light you are.

We also wish to touch on the concept of your physical body, for you are working within your physical vessel, and you will notice that your signal also gets dulled by the way in which you treat your body. Yes, you can amplify attraction by taking proper care of your physical body. Simply put, notice all of the things that lower your vibration, and in your world there is much to watch out for. To put it simply, toxins in your environment, water, skin and beauty products, cookware, furniture and other belongings affect your vibration, as do medications, perfumes, processed and refined foods, and anything else you're putting in or on your body that is not as close to its natural form as possible. It is to look at your overall intake of what has been altered by man, because everything in its natural state, from the earth, is what will keep you in your highest vibration. It is to notice the overall load of these things and see where you can reduce the intake, to keep your vibration as high as possible.

Many of you will notice the more and more you consume and use things that are in their purest, most natural form, your consciousness starts to shift, your vibration starts to shift, and your body starts to shift to be more and more in alignment with your energetic frequency. The more you detoxify your vessel, the brighter your light shines. Think of all of the toxins and processed foods as a layer of dirt covering a diamond. Clean the diamond and see how brightly it shines, and often, when the diamond is clean, it's even reminded itself of its own beauty that perhaps it had forgotten. You, dear one, are the diamond—allow yourself to shine. Supporting your physical vessel is one of the most tangible ways to raise your frequency, and we will also offer that supporting your physical vessel will be very different depending on you as an individual, as different bodies require different levels of support. Honor your body's unique needs at each time, and remember that your Mother Earth is always there to care for, nurture, and support you.

As you support your physical body and release relationships or patterns in your life that are no longer in alignment, you will see your world start to change, and from there things open up for you to fully be in creation.

part nine

Setting Intentions

We will speak more on intention, and different ways to set it. Know that we are listening, and there are many ways to add energy to an intention. Speak it out, write it out, let us know what it is you are setting your intention toward, and know that when you set an intention, it will come to you as long as you are in alignment with it and keep the intention clear. When this intention is for your soul's highest and best, it will come to you in the timeline that is based on something greater than what you can see, for we can see the twists and turns of your journey, and this is where it is crucial to trust that as it comes to you is so perfect in every which way and exactly what is best for you at some time. Realize that the pieces of your reality that have many moving parts might take longer, in your perception of time, than you might expect, and it is through this process that all is coming together perfectly for you, when it is at the best time for all. Understand that with manifestation, it can take "time" for others potentially involved to be in alignment, and there are many moving parts, as we have said, as different people are also setting their intentions, and energy shifts in and out as things are being created.

Sometimes what was the best note for the song before suddenly needs to be shifted for the song's best interest as the creation process continues on, because the energies have shifted, and so it is with your life as well. There is a beautiful dance between your energy and intention, free will, and that of others, in co-creating with the divine, and really working together with all of the energies of the One. A muscle in the body of one might want to grow in one way, but requires the support of surrounding muscles before reaching its fullest potential, and so it is similar with your growth and path.

Similarly, the process is working in different planes and dimensions, and pulling it into your unique time and dimension is slower than in higher frequencies. The more you raise your vibration and dance with the higher frequencies, you will notice that manifestation is effortless. In fact, much of your impatience around creation in your life, and things shifting, is because your soul knows that in other dimensions, your manifestations are instant, and how does this work?

When you dream something up, as you say, it is in existence. Perhaps not in the way that you define existence as something that is in very physical, 3D form, but if it wasn't available in the field it wouldn't be available for your "imagination," and this is how you can start to pull it into your dimension. And so, your daydreaming and night dreaming and allowing yourself to wander in your mind and imagination are helpful tools to explore your world of possibilities. Where have you been told this is wrong, childish, or a waste of time? Perhaps by the same forces that have kept you blocked from seeing the depth of your power to begin with—for what could you create if you knew you could create it all? If you fully understood that your energy is shifting everything around you?

This is what we are unlocking now, and you will notice that as you start to shift the world around you, and shift your vibration, you might notice a pushback of energy from people around you who are feeling the difference in your energy—for whenever we feel a difference in frequency, this can lead to a "triggering" feeling, depending on the person's perception. This is helpful for you to know in how people respond—this is a sign of your shift, reflected back to you, and also for you to know as you're faced with this yourself. Start to be in awareness as you move through the world of what feels incongruent with your current vibration. Where many of you miss out on large aspects of expansion is that you assume that the incongruence means they are not for you. And this is true in the moment— but what if that energy is expansive for you and in the direction you desire, rather than a frequency that you do not desire? It can go either way—it is up to you to discern the difference. What you perceive to be fear could also be excitement and expansion. Notice where you might confuse the two, and this is where approaching with curiosity and joy allows you to not skip over the leaps into higher vibrations. This is where what scares you the most can be what expands you the most.

In setting intention—speak it, write it, know it. It is a declaration, and it will come to you. When you are firm in your belief, there is no other way, and the longer you stay firm in that belief, that thing you are manifesting becomes so much a part of your identity, there is no other way than to receive it—for you are it. Where you over-ask is where you are unsure, and there is no need to be unsure if you are in knowing. If you are asking for it too often, rooted in being unsure if it's coming, then you are not rooted in the belief, and there is the underlying work to be done, shifts to be made.

If you do not believe that you are worthy of receiving the thing, if you do not believe it is possible, here again is another block, for if you are the frequency, how could it be possible that you would not believe it is possible? This would be to say that you are not possible! You are, of course, all possibility, if you allow yourself to see. And so, notice where you can shift into knowing that it is possible. If it is possible in your daydreams, it is possible—for it exists in the field, and now you are pulling it in. If it is possible for another, you have examples of how this is possible for you—you know the energies exist. But the most important way to know it is possible is to feel the frequency within yourself.

Whatever your intention is, why is it that you are setting your sights there? What are you looking to create in your life? What in your life already allows you to feel this way, or could make you feel this way instantaneously? The more you allow yourself to be in the emotions and already experience what you want, more physical manifestations of it will come to you. Be creative. Be love. Be free. Be happy. All of these high-frequency emotions allow you to attract what you want to you, they add amplification to the practice, but it is to realize that what you really want is in the now.

We know that many of you desire certain things because you believe it will make you feel a certain way, but sometimes it is not that thing that will allow you to feel a certain way. If you allow yourself to feel that way in the now, you will notice that it is not conditional—for all emotions are available to you at this time, all frequencies—so you can choose it in the now. Where you slow yourselves down is where you have set so many conditions and expectations on doing certain things and feeling certain things—this is where you slow it all down, and you are staying stuck in living in the old way—always looking to the past or the future, but the only moment that exists is the now. And so, why wait four years to feel a certain way when you can feel that way now? And perhaps the inner child in you says that you can't feel the way you want now because it's not in the way you want, but this is where you block yourself from happiness—you choose. And this leads us into our next offering, which is releasing the attachment.

When you set your intention on achieving or having something in particular, it is because you think it will allow you to feel a certain way, but what if it wouldn't at all? And so a way that you can ensure your manifestation will allow you to feel that way is to open the floor a bit for your Highest Self to create something even better. Perhaps you wish for a big house on the beach, but what if that big house on the beach actually was too windy and loud and didn't allow you the quiet that you needed, and if you moved into a house in the country, which you never would have wished for yourself initially, that was the thing that allowed you to feel free and happy and loved and supported? Are you open to something better?

This is where we will point out that to have more control over your own life, it is in fact for your ego to release control so that the divine, your highest aspects, can allow you to truly receive what is in your highest and best. Where your ego can keep you safe, it can also keep you small, and you will learn to trust the higher aspects of yourself that are fully in love to create things that are the miracles you are ready to activate. And when we invite you to give an idea, but to allow things to shift along the way, what does this bring up in you? What is in the resistance? It is so often at this part in the journey that there is resistance, and you block yourself yet again.

part ten
Receiving and Releasing Attachment

We will remind you of deep programming that life is meant to be hard, and that only through hard work comes good things. We say yes and no to this, for there are many ways to achieve amazing things, and what are the "good things" that these people speak of? Are they things *you* want, or things others do? Is that told to you by someone who is truly happy, or someone who has worked hard and doesn't want to believe it was all for nothing? Where are you so blindly trusting of people around you, who say things that feel true, yet you do not trust yourself—your own thoughts, your own desires, and your soul itself? Isn't it interesting where you don't trust your Soul, your higher guidance that unconditionally loves you, yet there might be so many places where you trust those who are in lower frequencies, who might not be in happiness themselves, and who are outside of you? This is where you trust another's discernment above your own, but the key to your happiness is to learn to truly trust yourself first and foremost, which you will unravel the more you realize that as you take leaps that are purely in alignment, you are able to create what others who are limited to "what makes sense" based on their programs of illusions do not.

We invite you to know that you are so loved, so supported—we are always looking to support you — will you allow us? How we see it is similar to looking for help on a piece of homework, and instead of asking the teacher who will readily give you support, you turn to a student next to you and see what they wrote down. We invite you to look into your programs around those who are older than you, those who taught you, whether that be teachers, parents, supporters—and where did you perhaps learn that those who were supposed to support you actually did not? Where did you learn to be let down by support, and thus not trust who was meant to be supportive?

We love you so much, dear one, and we are here to support you in ways far beyond what you allow yourselves to imagine. And so this is to dive into your relationship with receiving support. You can see your divine helpers, the energies all around you, as your mother, father, advisor, teacher, supporter in all aspects. The One is all around you, with you, within you, supporting you, as it supports itself. The same way your body is created to work in harmony, all the pieces together—it wants to sustain life, it works as hard as it can to do this. Do you allow yourself to receive support?

Where you force yourself to believe you must do it alone, or that you cannot trust supporters, might be where you are not following the signs. We show them everywhere. Can you believe that we are always in support? Where do you not believe you are worthy of support? Where do you have programs that if it is not difficult, it is not worth it? This is again where you believe there are certain conditions to feeling what you want to feel, to feeling the state of achievement. It is where you add resistance to the flow because you decide there needs to be resistance. Where are you choosing to add resistance to the flow of things? This is where you make it harder for yourself, you don't allow there to be an easier way, you're not open to support in different dimensions and in your now. There is no need to add extra resistance, for the feeling will be just as sweet if it flows to you, and it comes sooner, if you are ready to experience the blissful feeling and highest vibrations possible for you not in the *future* but in the now, which is all that truly exists anyway.

And if you are thinking that you are not adding anything to make it harder than it should be, but it feels *hard* to get there, well there is the sign to swap out the puzzle piece or to twist it around, to step back and see a wider range of possibilities. Remember that you can ask your Highest Self to drop in a sign of how to do or see things in a different way, and follow the signs. But where you are pushing too hard is where you are being given guidance.

We will give you this example—imagine you are in a long hallway with a number of doors on either side, all closed, and you set your clear intention to go to the room that contains the key to your happiness. In that moment, all of the doors that do not lead you to the key to your happiness are immediately locked, so that you are guided to the correct door, but you forgot you were told this would happen. You do remember that you've seen others walk the hallway before, and you have some beliefs around which door you should be going to. You are also very curious and believe you know the correct door. As you try door after door and they are locked, you get frustrated. Some doors you keep jangling at, and you cannot get them open, and you get frustrated. At a certain point, you are so convinced the key to your happiness is behind a specific door, you knock it down with all of your force and might after kicking it multiple times, and you enter. What you were seeking isn't there—it's a letdown, and perhaps you give up, or perhaps you keep going down the hallway, seeing what doors you can open.

Where you get frustrated at the locked doors and try to force them open is where you are in resistance to the path, and where you don't allow yourself to be guided in the easiest, most effortless way to exactly what you want. For if you spent your time simply checking what was locked and then moving on, you would make your way to the unlocked door more quickly, and be on your merry way. And so, where you try to force your way through is where you are not listening to the guidance.

This is not to say, however, that there are not challenges along your path that allow you to grow, and we invite you to start to truly discern the difference between a challenge or obstacle that allows you to step into a higher version of yourself, versus living in the resistance, for they are different energies that can be easily confused. As you approach what you perceive to be a challenge, you are given an opportunity to expand your energy of solutions, your awareness of possibilities, and expand your consciousness even more, showing yourself that you are capable of more, as you truly always are, and then you are onto the next.

These experiences are much of what allows for your growth as a human, and are what you "signed up" for, and you can perceive them as obstacles in the most exciting, most fun obstacle course your soul specifically designed for you, or you can see them as things getting in your way. This is quite a different energy than pushing hard the whole way through, noticing that deep down there is a nonresonance the whole time, feeling like you are trudging through life with a heavy weight tied around your ankles—for that is not your purpose in this life! You are here to feel light and free and allow yourself to float through, and when you hit a *point* of resistance, you are able to transmute, shift, feel, or redirect back onto the aligned path again, allowing the river to take you along in the way you'd like, but noticing where the riverbank is turning you around, as opposed to trying to swim up the current the whole way through.

Where is it that you fear surrender? Why does surrender perhaps have a negative connotation in society? Again, we will remind you to notice where you have assigned connotations to words based on programming without deciding for yourself. We offer to you that surrender is the release of resistance, of force, and underneath this is a reminder that perhaps your life was not meant to be forced the whole way through—can you allow yourself to be in joy? What do you believe will occur if you are in joy instead of hardship? Where do you find that people in your life only bond from the difficulties, that you only feel supported in the difficulties? But what if there is support in the expansion and beauty and happiness?

Surrender is trust, surrender is love. It is misguided to believe that trust in the highest, purest frequencies of expansion would lead you astray. Where do you believe there is glory in the struggle along the way? When you admire the energy of another—is it the process itself, or what they achieve in the end—and what if this could be achieved without the struggle? What we will offer to you, that might hit a nerve for some—but we know you understand we are dedicated to the embodiment of truth—is that so often the struggle is glorified and focused on simply to allow those who are currently struggling, as a means to achieving, to feel better about themselves. And while we are not saying there is anything inherently wrong with struggle energy, for there is much growth in this process, if that perception is allowed, it is to be honest with yourself about where you are allowing yourself to go down a more difficult path, trying to force what you think has to be done, and justifying it by seeing others around you in it, when again, you cannot be sure of how they are truly feeling or how effective or efficient their creation process is.

Where you are in the energy of comparison is where you are not in alignment with your soul, for there is no need to compare when everything you have and will ever want is within you, and to compare yourself to another is also to compare yourself to yourself, which wouldn't be productive at all—for you are all part of the same One. And you will notice the more you are energetically supportive, loving, excited for, and uplifting of others, you feel these energies sent back to you in beautiful, powerful ways. As you are embodying them, you magnify them back to you, and on a larger scale, where you uplift another is where you uplift yourself, as they are reflections of you, an energetic attachment to you, and where, quite simply, your body is feeling that same energy.

This is where you might hear your saying of "treat people as you want to be treated"—you see this play out as energies are sent back to you by others, but it is that you are treating yourself a certain way as you treat others a certain way. And so if you are in a high-frequency relationship with another, this is also reflective of a high-frequency relationship with yourself. When you say loving words to another, as you say "I love you, always and forever," and you feel that vibration in your body, your body is filled with this frequency, even if directed to another, and now you are filled with this love one and the same. And so we see overlap in how we communicate, what we attract, and of course what we are, for it is all of the same.

To surrender is not to give up, but to allow yourself to be effortlessly realigned with your intention. If you are clear and your beliefs align with your intention, of course it is coming to you, and you let the timing play out as it might, and you let the way in which it comes to you be beautiful and magical and miraculous. When you try to plan it out ahead of time is where you might block the magic—and what a great story if it comes to you in an exciting way that you couldn't have ever dreamed of! Many of you ask for miracles, yet you want to plan them out—well then, you don't perceive it to be a miracle when it comes! Think of the excitement in a magic show—not knowing what's next, not knowing how it comes, but knowing that something fun and interesting and miraculous is coming up next. This is how you can see your life, and you are the main character in a beautiful play of miracles—it is your only job to be open to receiving.

We communicate to you about where there is force, for if things are being made difficult the whole way through, this is where the frequencies do not match, and your supportive guides are guiding you to look through another door, to make a shift. And when it feels like flow is when you know it is the right place, and you keep flowing until there is perhaps another shift to make, and this is the beauty of co-creation—it does not need to be a struggle the whole way through. As you create the most beautiful song to ever be shared, perhaps you get a bit tired, or get stuck for a moment, but the journey is one of excitement and fun and creativity and joy and inspiration and, of course, flow. Let yourself be inspired, and let yourself notice where things are not as you wish—are you trying to force something that perhaps is not for your best? Allow your soul to steer you to where you can be in happiness in the now.

Your attachment is another form of resistance, energetically speaking, and by attachment we mean where you are so tied to the outcome, the when, the how, any aspect of that which you want coming in, that you perhaps block the process in a number of ways. Remember that what is meant for you will come to you. What is a vibrational match and in alignment with your highest comes to you. Your intention is powerful. Where you are overly attached is where you are in the belief that if it does not happen, or if it does not happen when or how you want, you will not be free, happy, content, successful or whatever other energy you're looking to embody, but this is where you do not believe in yourself, trust in yourself, and really we mean trust in your Soul and the higher frequencies, where you do not trust in the universe, the energy around you—but the truth is that that is all there is.

Where you notice your attachment is your opportunity to dig deeper and undo any knots that have been tied to beliefs that limit your expansion. This could be a form of keeping yourself small. This could be a form of your ego trying to maintain control because it does not want to be overridden, and it is afraid of the unknown, but the unknown is all that you've been hoping to remember and experience.

It is an interesting thing to discuss the unknown—you can perceive it as what is unknown, or you can perceive it as everything, all that is known, and that your energy has access to all of this but you simply pull down specific pieces at a time. And through such, it is more in what you have experienced in this incarnation and what you have remembered that is the known, and everything else simply hasn't been accessed for it isn't in alignment, and it's not so scary then, is it? The ego is the piece of yourself to integrate, and to not allow to run the ship. You can take the information, but allow your Highest Self to guide the way—it is simply a piece of information.

We again return to the question of, why the attachment? Why must it happen that way? Where you try to force it in a single way is where you resist the flow, is where you decide perhaps to make it more of a struggle than you need, is where you have decided that your ego knows more than your soul, is where you are not open to what is miraculous coming to you. It is time to stop limiting yourself, dear one! There is so much available to you!

When you are in the energy of, "I want it *now*, I *need* it *now*," now you feel into the vibration of the younger version of you that didn't feel listened to, didn't feel provided for, didn't feel safe. Rest into the knowing that you are safe, you are provided for, and where you are operating from energies of the opposite is where you start to see evidence in your environment of the opposite. Where you are in attachment is where you resist collaboration, and this is where you can tune into the programs around collaboration and what that meant in your past—the belief that you must do it yourself and plan it out for it to be done correctly, but this is operating from fear energy, and is where, in fact, you do not attract it in. These are all energies to reflect on, and notice where they come up in you.

part eleven

Authenticity

Set your intention and know it will be delivered. There is not a question, and it will be delivered in the most miraculous way. Because you know it will be delivered, you have it. You have ordered the new couch, and now it is time to create space for the couch and get things sorted for when it arrives. You already have the couch, so you can plan the party for Saturday knowing it is here—do you see what we are getting at? How does your energy shift when you know you have the couch? It is not to wait until you receive the thing to feel a certain way, but to show up as that person today. Again, this is where you have been taught, unknowingly, to limit yourself, as you believe there are stepping stones to feeling ready. And then at some point, you realize that one of the greatest illusions of them all is that you have to wait to be ready to do what you want and be who you want, that you have to wait for approval from anyone outside of yourself to be who you want to be, and that even those who you view as most "expert" might feel a bit of nerves or fear (really just excitement!) before they jump in, but they are confident in who they are, and so they move forward, and you do not have to wait for anything to get there.

And so, when you have the love you always wanted, the home you always wanted, the job you always wanted, when you write the book, sing in front of the crowd, or achieve any other aspirations you might have set your sights on, how will you feel? What will your energy be like? It is similar to how you perceive birthdays. Do you feel different on your birthday, waking up one year older? As you get older, you realize that your birthday doesn't necessarily feel different, even if it did when you were younger. You realize that it is arbitrary, where your society decided to celebrate when you were born, and then there were standard rituals to acknowledge your existence, and that certain ages decide certain liberties you have—but again, this is all arbitrary. What you are allowed to do at the age of eighteen, perhaps, is based on an assumption of maturity that you know is not realized for all, yet at this age you receive more privileges.

As an example, let's say the day you turn eighteen is the day that is standard in your society to move out and live on your own. It's the day you turn eighteen—do you really feel ready? For some, perhaps, but others not. Either way, it is time to do it. Knowing that you are doing it is where you decide to make the energetic shift to align with it, and you suddenly grow into a new level of maturity that was required for you to successfully support yourself. On your wedding day, why is it that some get cold feet? How is it that perhaps you are so sure in your knowing of love, but there are pieces of you that have doubts? Maybe they are signs, maybe they are your ego, maybe it is your vibration catching up to you. These are instances where action and frequency are forced to align, and we offer these examples to you so that you can see it is all in choice.

When you set your intention, you are in knowing that you are in creation. Knowing, not hope or belief. You are being thrown into the ring—it is done. And so, in this moment you decide to prepare yourself by allowing your frequency to match up with that, to step into this higher version of yourself, and to take action in alignment with it already happening, for it has, it is here. Remember that the universe acts based on energetic feedback. The energies you attract in are shifting in response to what you are.

And so, if you set your intention that you will feel pure true love, but your actions are not consistent with this, the universe understands this as an updated intention, and so it is in response to that. And when you send mixed messages, there is no propelling forward into what you want, immediately. And truly, what we are trying to get at is supporting you in truly creating instantaneous shifts, which are absolutely possible when you realize that you can wake up one day and be a new person, that you can be a new person in the next hour, in the next minute, in the next second. This is available to you. You can decide that when you wake up on your next birthday you feel different—but realize this is totally arbitrary, it is just easier for you to justify shifting your perception if you can pair it with turning thirty or forty or fifty. Similarly, the idea of New Year's resolutions is simply a justification of making an identity shift—but we will remind you that you need permission from no one else to utilize your power as a multidimensional, ever-expanding being, and you can shift your identity whenever you want.

Why so many of you do not shift your identities is because you look for feedback from those around you to tell you who you are, or to tell you that it is okay, but this is where it is backward—the external feedback will adjust to who you show up as and declare to be, and you will alway make faster shifts working with your own energy than waiting around for someone else to shift theirs! For example, you could meet three new people for every meal of the day and tell the first that you are very creative, tell the second you are very athletic, and tell the third you are lazy. Each will see you as what you expressed, and believe this about you, perceiving you from the framework you offered. Yet, if you tell someone you are very extroverted but they only observe you being quiet and shy, they will not believe that you are an extrovert.

Energy speaks louder than words. And so, what are you telling the universe you are? How are you showing up? This is what energies around you respond to.

Another block to shifting identity is worry about how others will respond—*what will they say? Will they believe me? Will they cast me out?* And this is where your mind gets in the way of your expansion, and where you give your power of creation away and limit yourself based on projections of others. Remember, this all points back to trust in yourself and remembrance of your right to be who you want.

Another deeper program that often comes up is believing that you have to be how you are told you are or what you should be, and we ask, why do you hang onto this when you know there is so much more available to you? Anywhere you are not being your truest self is where you block your frequency, and to emit a clear signal of magnetism, you must be in alignment with who you are. And when we discuss showing up and acting as the person who already has what you want, if this feels like a shift in identity to you, we invite you to ask yourself—is it a shift in identity to someone I am not? Or is it actually a shift in identity to allow me to step into the highest, truest version of myself—perhaps a version of myself that is so clear, bright, true and aligned, that for so long I felt was too bright to be seen? Illuminate yourself.

Showing up as the truest version of yourself allows you to fully breathe, to release the weight off your shoulders, and this is the only way to magnetize all of the miracles that are always available to you. It is authenticity that makes you powerfully magnetic. Where are you not fully in your authenticity? What is authentic feels good—it is a knowing in your soul. The old programs you might have about yourself that feel low frequency are not in fact your authentic self—for if they were, they would not feel incongruent, lower vibration, "not good" to you.

You can shift your frequency any time you choose with conscious intention, and this goes hand in hand with taking action that aligns with you already having what you want to have. For if you are calling in your dream home that allows you to feel rooted, grounded, and safe, take a few minutes to loosen yourself and allow that energy to fill you up. You are rooted, grounded, and safe. Feel it fully in your body. And as someone who is fully rooted, grounded, and safe, it is time for you to move through your world, and all of the actions you take and choices you make come from that energy of being fully rooted, grounded, and safe, and thus you take action in alignment with what you want, because you already have it, because you already are it, and you feel how you wanted to feel, and the physical manifestation will arrive shortly. It is simple if you allow it to be.

part twelve

Feeling Your Emotions

Notice where you overcomplicate the practice of manifesting abundant things into your life, another example of living from the program that it all has to be achieved through struggle. This is another place where so many believe that "manifestation" is "too good to be true," because they block out what could make things peaceful or easier along the way, but the irony is that they are already manifesting. If you are already working with the tools, we believe it is best not to do so blindly! However, it is a choice. And we hope that you can see this clearly now—that you have so many more possibilities and choices than you think, and the more you practice, the more you will start to work with them.

With the arrival of the physical manifestations, we will return to releasing attachment, which goes along with being at peace with all of the timelines. When you are at peace with the many ways in which things can drop in and occur, there is no need to be attached. You might ask, *how can I be at peace with all of the timelines?* Well, dear one, we return to ego, and where your ego has already selected just a few potential timelines for you to tap into, these are based on probability, perhaps, but also or instead based on the programs you are running that are influencing what possibilities are brought into your awareness. If you could accurately see the infinite timelines available to you, and understand how they consistently shift and change, because you are the creator, then you could put your mind at ease. But part of why you signed up for this experience was to not know all of the timelines at once, for that would take the fun and growth out of the game. And suddenly you wouldn't feel the essence of progression that your Soul desired when it chose to come here, for not knowing all allows us to learn lessons—patience is a lesson, peace is a lesson, and this is part of your experience. Every step is beautiful and miraculous and wonderful.

We point this out because we understand that for many, they worry because they have a specific timeline in mind, but realize that what you are worrying about is what you are radiating with your energy body, and what you are focusing on, and as that signal is emitted, now you perhaps add more momentum to a timeline you didn't want in the first place. And the idea that only two timelines are possible is very limited and where you are stuck in ego and the processing of your human brain, but you are so much more vast than this! When you notice worry about a timeline popping up, you are free to say "no thank you," and instead allow yourself to daydream about what you do desire to happen.

Many of you worry about things that might happen, thus drawing it to you—for this is the energy you are focusing on. And where you are focused on *not* focusing on something is also where you are focusing on it, and so all you need to do is say, "no thank you," like seeing a "dead end" sign on a street and simply choosing to take a different road, rather than steering the car onto the dead-end street and worrying about what you'll do when you get to the end of it.

You will notice a similar energy pop up when you are facing "tests," as you call them, where you can find yourself dropping into worry, overanalyzing, wondering what it means, feeling defeated, and so on. Before creating more stories about what it means or could mean, we invite you to continue to tune into your heart and drop into your pure knowing, for you *do* know, dear one, what is fully aligned with you, as a being of pure love. It is from this space that you will find clarity—in the pure love of your heart, and it is this that you can use as the set point of frequencies you come across. When the "test" arises, you will notice your energetic resilience in how you respond, and in fact, it is an opportunity to strengthen this muscle. When the "test" arises, do you immediately fall into fear or worry? Again, then what are you magnetizing?

Allow yourself to feel your emotion, but cradle it with love, and remind it that you need to focus on that (love) if the current emotion is not the energy you want to anchor in. This is where you can allow the emotion to be fully felt, and facilitate its leaving of the body, and then anchor in how you want to feel. Affirm the knowing that is in alignment with your Soul. We remind you again, dear one, that you are love, and what is of fear is therefore not your permanent truth. When the "tests" arise, this is your opportunity to clear out any energies of fear, doubt, or insecurity. If you respond to the "test" with any low-frequency energies, you will know it is somewhere within your system, and your awareness will allow you to gain even more awareness around the root of the emotion so you can reperceive the root, and then move out the energy so it no longer magnetizes more of its kind.

Moving out the energies can be done in a few ways, and you will feel it as it leaves your body, which might not be all at once. And we will reaffirm, it is not to avoid low-frequency emotions if they come, for this is to be in your humanness, but to notice where they become stuck in your system, as this can affect what you magnetize. You can move out these energies through intentional movement (setting intention before movement to clear the energy), through energy healing or energy work, through crying, screaming, dancing, letters, jumping, stretching, yoga, breathwork, and so on. Remember that intentionality charges everything, and there are many practices you can utilize to move emotions through. But the key is to allow yourself to feel them without judgment, and it is through this practice that your body learns again that it is safe to feel, safe to be held, and always loved—not conditionally based on thoughts that pass through, experiences that don't go as expected, or emotions felt.

part thirteen
Following the Signs

And now we will move on to following the signs, for as we have discussed, the universe will flow with you. You will receive signs that are like clues, leading you to the next step in more and more things opening up in your life. As you continue to raise your vibration, you will notice that your life begins to feel like a beautiful, joyful treasure hunt, and almost as if you find treasure in your life every bit along the way.

So, what do these "signs" look like? They can come through in many ways, as we communicate in many ways, and by "we," it is to start to understand even more that we are aspects of you, different frequencies of you that of course are always in support and guidance and love. The clues we leave for you need not be searched for, however, for you will notice them if you are simply aware that they might be there. And so, after you set your intention, be the vibration, and act from the vibration, you let go, and let the rest fall into place, noticing where you are led. You can ask for signs along the way, and this is where your intuition will pop up and guide you in which direction to go if you hit a fork in the road. A way we send signs is the flow we have discussed before, and where heavy resistance comes up, there is another, easier way. We send signs through others, in perhaps a message they share with you or that you overhear, through music, through numbers, through books, through street signs, through whispers in your heart, through your gut instinct, through animals—the ways are infinite.

When it comes to following the clues, all you need to do is be open to what could lead you where, while it might not make logical sense to your logical brain, this is where you are learning to work with flow, and how those who live their lives in flow already notice that things drop into their laps, for they are always following the flow of things and simultaneously the universe is dropping in what is in alignment with their frequency. Release judgment of the clues, for all is valuable, and often we show you signs or symbols simply so you know you are on the right path, and that we are in support. Where you read too much into the symbol is where you switch over into your logical brain again, which is important to become aware of in case you find that your logic entices you to second guess, and then entices you to stop trusting yourself. The key is to be in awareness.

We hear the question, "What does it mean?" again and again, and we ask you—how does it make you feel? Again, tune into your heart, into your intuition, and you will know exactly what it means. It is a wave from us, a nudge of support, a reminder that you are in alignment and we are working with you. And over time perhaps you will develop a unique style of communication with us that will become stronger and stronger, and you will become more confident in following the clues, especially as the miracles drop in—for you can see miracles every day if you allow yourself to. There is magic all around, love all around, but what is it that you focus on?

And we will speak more to this, another point of confusion—it is not simply a single thought that shifts everything, but what you spend attention on is what is mostly in your field, and again, it is the energy of what you're spending attention on that the field around you is noticing, and what you spend more energy thinking about is what you add more energy to. And this allows it to grow, and momentum is added to the timeline where it manifests physically in your life. We note this so you start to notice what you focus your attention on, and really we invite you to focus on the energy of it rather than the words themselves, for this will give you a clearer idea of what is being energized and amplified.

For example, if you want to find a romantic partner, and you keep thinking about how you don't have a partner and how much you want one, the frequency underneath this is one of lack, and one of being alone. However, you could simply switch this so you're not amplifying the energy of lack, and instead that of true love, feeling safe, confident, secure, loved, and loving. When this is what is felt and magnetized in your body, you will receive more of that abundance and fullness. As you have heard many times, it is to focus on what you want, rather than what you don't. And again, the key energy or emotion will be the most important thing to focus on, to fully feel in your body in order to amplify it and call in a physical manifestation of it.

part fourteen

Channeling
Your Emotions

We will add extra attention to our note of *feeling* it in your body, not simply thinking about it, for there is a difference. You can think about feeling love all day long, but you will notice a profound difference when you feel that vibration—energize the vibration, not the word itself. What are words but a way to express a vibration? But they are not always the vibration themselves. This is when you call them "empty words"—when someone says something but there is no emotion behind it, and then what does it really mean at all? The word can help to evoke the emotion, which is why it is a powerful tool, but we will also remind you that you don't need a word to describe the vibration of what you want to call in. It can simply be the feeling that you can feel in your body, and you know what it is associated with.

So perhaps you are unsure of what the word is for the feeling is you want to have, which is why you truly want something, but perhaps you can take a moment to visualize having the thing, and the emotion you associate with it, and realize that it is that vibration you're feeling in your body that is the most powerful tool for magnetizing in what you want, and this is available to you at all times. Emotions are available to all. They are one of the greatest gifts of the human experience, and you will start to uncover how the things that perhaps you believed, or others believed, made you weak are actually the foundation for some of your greatest, most enchanting gifts.

We also see, however, that some struggle to fully feel emotion, and we wish to address this. Again, release any judgment, for your body will feel what it is made safe to feel, and the more you open up space for emotions to come through in a gentle, loving space and manner, you can learn to feel emotions again. And so, with emotions we see the contrast that is such a great teacher, for when you feel the lowest lows, you are able to feel more deeply the highest highs, and this is in fact why people who feel their emotions so deeply can more easily call into their lives what they desire, if they understand how to channel their energy in that direction.

Why is it that so many dull their emotions and don't allow themselves to fully feel? The intensity, the discomfort, and feeling the power of frequency in the body. It is a wonder to you how something that is not in the physical, something that does not have a solid, tangible form can be so incredibly powerful, and is of, within, and through you. If your emotions have the power to make you cry, to evoke a physical response in you, to make you shift your behavior and your life, imagine how you can channel the intensity of your emotions in the direction you want—supercharging the highest frequencies of joy, laughter, love, and fun, and using those to amplify more physical manifestations of what you desire into your life. Notice how what seems to break your heart is a reminder of its capacity to feel, and so often, actually depends on its capacity to feel the intensity of emotions. The greater this capacity, the more deeply and purely you can also feel the highest emotions, and this can be a great advantage for you as you learn to channel this energy in the direction that you want, rather than moving through life always using a tool that you were never aware you were even holding!

The more fun you have, the more you bring this into your life, and this we wish to point to even more clearly, because it is a simple yet powerful practice to incorporate into your daily life that will completely shift your vibration and allow you to keep integrating versions of your younger self that have so much magic within them. How would a child play? Notice the excitement, the joy, the creativity. There are no rules, only fun and what feels good. There is no pressure, you create as you go, and there are no mistakes. There is always something new you can create to shift the situation. This is the truest energy of "problem solving" that is effective, but it has been lost because so many have shut off their inspiration and curiosity, and instead, or so heavily, locked into "thinking it out," which has its merit. But we are curious how many of you would feel if you utilized all aspects of yourselves rather than just the few that you have been taught to focus on.

There is so much remembering that takes place through this process, and a level of the remembering is who you were as a child, and really who you are, for this is within you, and how can you be that purest energy of yourself—so innocent, so excited, so curious, knowing that you could change the world, be anything, allowing yourself to dream. Think of the energy of daydreaming, one of the simplest tools for co-creating your life that you can use, and it is so simple! Notice the state that you're in, energetically and with your brain, as you daydream— it allows you to float. Do you notice how in the daydream you are free? There is no resistance! Anything is possible! How can you add more of this energy to your own life? How can you play? Do you know how to play? We encourage you to try on different types of playing, and this is a beautiful way to support others in raising their frequency as well, if you play with others! Whenever you wish for bigger shifts, or faster shifts, drop into your fun muscle, build it up, and see all that bubbles up from it! This is where the intuition drops in, this is where you embody love and joy and creativity and play, and you are ready to receive what is coming to you.

With fun, you will notice that you start to feel full yourself, full on love and happiness, for these high-frequency energies quite literally fill your body, and you are satiated in new ways. In this fullness, there is contentment—it is fullness in your life—peace. And you will notice that you have even more to give, more to share, and no longer coming from a place of sacrificing your own happiness, using your energy to give to others, but now from the knowing that there is more than enough for everyone, for love is an unlimited resource, as everything is of love, all energy can be transmuted. This is the difference in your style of giving, for this is where you will fill yourself up and give to others, rather than feeling depleted yourself in giving to others. It can be both, and in fact, the more you fill yourself up, the more you have more for others, and this is how you spread more and more love, but it all starts with you.

If you feel your love bucket is only halfway full and you pour what you have into another's, you will empty again, but if you fill your bucket so much that there is enough to fill another, now you will fill yours and those around you, and so we will tell you that it is not "selfish," in the way you believe, to fill yourself first. The word "selfish" is an interesting one, and you can either choose a different word or untangle the connotations you might have associated with the word in order to understand our message here. Where you are made to feel guilty for filling yourself up is not coming from a place of love and understanding. Guilt is a low frequency that can then breed other low-frequency situations and emotions, and you are strong enough to know the power of your vibration and what is truly in alignment with who you are. You are not here to feel guilty all the time, and certainly not about caring for yourself and giving yourself love. Without giving yourself full love, how is it that you can fully love any other, and how is it that you will be giving from the highest frequency possible?

Focusing on things out of order is what has led so many of you to feel burnt out, exhausted, and like you are "not allowed" to play, have fun, or enjoy. We ask you—whose rules are these? Who instituted them? Where are you tying your own hands and making yourself feel guilty for playing? What is it you feel about yourself if you make time for play? This is really where we get to the root of it, because it is either fear of what others think or perhaps fear of what will happen to you or even what you will think of yourself. Either way, the energy underneath this is fear. We will remind you that true play and having fun, tuning into the energy in its purest form, is not at the expense of anyone, but truly a lightening of the energy, being in joy, and also in alignment with loving yourself. Where the idea of "fun" has been misconstrued and is not in fact the vibration of what we are talking about is if the activities you have assigned as "fun" are connected to lower vibrational thoughts or actions in relation to you or any other, for this is not purely in love, and what we are tuning into is being your true essence— which is love.

When you feel "stuck," this is where you might have lost the play, the enjoyment, the fun, and we invite you to embrace your childlike self, as it is always within you. Remember that this is a spark that will always turn on your magic again, and this is where the purest, most innocent, lovely relations will be built from. It is funny how so many of the things you are made to be in adulthood make it so you forget your childlike wonder and innocence, but you will find so many answers when you allow yourself to remember your childlike state— what you loved, what you didn't, your natural inclinations, your joys, your hopes, your dreams, and the simple goal to be in fun always. What was it like to play?! This is an important muscle to build again! The more you are in it, the more you will see how co-creation is effortless, fluid, because you are fully aligned with your innate essence as a creator.

For here is another layer of resistance—you are innately a co-creator, creating all the time, and so if you are also holding onto the belief that you are not a creator, and you're not acting in accordance, your system feels this dissonance, and your shine is dulled, your signals are confused, and you see how your magnetism is not as strong or quick as you might like, as you perceive it in your lower vibrational form. Why is it that being childish has a negative connotation? This is where the judgment comes in, the way of controlling you, making you feel like an outcast if you are being in curiosity and fun and play, and while there is balance of responsibility and fun, it is to realize that you can be both, you can be all, and that you do not have to sacrifice your joy and play for also being responsible and taking care. You are cared for, and you can also take care. In this process we hope you see how expansive you are, how multidimensional in every sense of the word, and that you are able to open yourself up not only to many more possibilities in your choices, but also in who you are, how you be, and again, that this can shift in any moment.

Where you might resist again is where the topic of identity comes up, for what is it to have an identity? We will tune into the frequency of the word, and we know that many on your planet have believed it to be something that is consistent and fixed, and who decided that? What is that which you identify with and as—and who is to say this cannot expand, change, or grow? This is your choice. But it is interesting how you think having a fixed identity will make you feel rooted, and in a sense is where you identify with your Soul, and know clearly what makes you feel most in alignment, and where you find yourself more and more, but what else do you associate identity with? There are bits of its essence that are mixed with alignment, but we also caution you to not box yourself in. For when you connect with your soul, you will see the magic unfold, but when you use identity as a way to keep yourself the same, to not be in exploration, or to be in the limitation that your current experience is all there is, now you miss out on the magic of life!

And if you are so tied to your identity, but you are attempting to call in something that is not in alignment with that identity, then you will feel stuck. And so, it is in shifting what you identify as to be a match for what you want to call in that is the key. But in order to do this is the necessary step of shifting your beliefs around identity—and what fears you might have around shifting it, and when that is allowed, what that means, what the conditions are, as we have discussed before. What is interesting is so many of you are so much more connected to your souls (what we think most of you want to connect to when you say "identity") as children, but then you get on the path of obligation and acting out of guilt or fear, following the path that you are told to follow, and then you "lose" yourself in it, and you might spend your whole life trying to "find" yourself again (really, a remembering of an expanded concept), exactly who you were connected to as a child (self-connection), and so this is one version of your Circle of Life.

To take time to remember yourself in your energy of childhood might give you much more clarity than you think. As a child, you knew how to listen to yourself, what you enjoyed and what you didn't, but you also didn't feel limited in expansion, you allowed yourself to explore and change and shift. And maybe you wore a different costume every day, and you enjoyed it. It was still in resonance. You took on a different "identity" every day in that sense, but it was still in congruence because your soul connection was strong and firm, and this is what anchored you in. For so many of you are looking for rooting, grounding, and stability, as you feel the shifts all around you. Where is it that you tie a rope to the riverbed because you are afraid of floating down the stream?

part fifteen

Energetic Flexibility

The fastest manifestors are the ones who allow themselves to change the most quickly—and to allow yourself to is simply a choice. But where you resist change is where you resist receiving what you want, for if it is not already in your awareness, it is because your energy hasn't attracted it in, and therefore it will require an energetic shift, or change, to attract it in, otherwise you wouldn't feel the need to switch at all. And so, can you allow yourself to get comfortable with change? With trying new things? With showing up in a different way?

This is energetic flexibility as we will call it—you are building energetic resilience as a muscle, and now we offer to you energetic flexibility, of how you can become so flexible with your frequency than you can adapt to meet any frequency you require at the time, and this allows you to dance with the frequencies all around you, and to become a master harmonizer. This is at the root of it all—becoming a master harmonizer!

When you learn to let yourself harmonize with the energies around you, you will see how quickly your physical reality shifts. Notice where you have become inflexible and stiff. The same way this limits the movement ability of your physical body, it limits the shifting of your frequency, and when you have the ability to stretch to the highest of frequencies, then you can naturally shift to be in alignment with that which you want, and you see the dance of effortless manifestation.

We will speak more to the practice of manifestation, and where it isn't necessary. Many in your society have learned manifestation as a step-by-step process, and if you wish to distill it down in this way and it makes you feel good and you are in happiness, then beautiful! But what we offer to you is that you really don't *need* any "steps" or to consciously "do" anything when you have shifted your consciousness and raised your vibration—everything else falls into place. And this is where manifesting what you want—shifting your outer reality—is an inside job as they say—for it is within yourself that you will find all of the keys and the codes. And if you simply allow yourself to be in your truest, highest state, if you drop resistance, live your life in a state of flow, in congruence with your design, in love for yourself and all, if you are open and flexible, if you allow yourself to play in life, and that is the way you *be*, everything else naturally falls where it is meant to, and your vibration is so high that you need not worry about what will happen or how it will happen or what it will do or what you "should" do. This is all chatter of the mind that has not yet been soothed or comforted, the busy mind that is still on the hamster wheel of programs and not yet connected to itself as Source, as the highest frequency of all, because as you connect with your true essence, you see the world magically, and everything else flows. When you are in your purest state of connection, you will naturally do what is in alignment with receiving what you want, and it is not something you will have to think about.

Thinking—let's discuss this more! Many of you are caught within your bodies because you overthink, and what is the root of this? Where did you learn that thinking would solve your problems? You know the answer to that, it is so deeply institutionalized, of course this is what you learned. And again, you realize how deeply the conditioning runs, so deeply that you do not even realize it's there. It is a rabbit hole you can go down, but not to worry. As you are in this process, allow that to all drop away, for you need not consciously know all of the programs you wish to let go of in order to do so, but rather it is to start unraveling the ball of yarn, and as you unravel one knot more start to naturally loosen, and then you can decide what you wish to knit with it. But what we are doing is unraveling the yarn, and then you will be on your merry way to knitting the most beautiful creation of all, even though it might turn into something else as you go. Remember to have fun with it!

When it comes to thinking, we ask you to not confuse this discussion for telling you thinking is "bad"—for while we can discuss those concepts, nothing is "good" or "bad" as we see it—it simply is. And our hope is that the more you see what is there, the more you are empowered by your ability to choose, when you see all that is there, you see what you can choose, you remember that you are always creating. And we are taking what has been automatic and out of conscious awareness and bringing it into your awareness—unlocking more and more for you along the way! But where the divine inspiration comes in is through the receiving of the information, and we will tell you that thinking is not the only way to solve the problem. Thinking is limited in the options that your brain will offer to you, as discussed, biased based on knowledge and beliefs. But when you tap into your cosmic source of information, you have many more solutions available to you, and you can allow them to drop in, or come through, rather than forcing or searching.

It is funny how so many of you search—it is like looking for your sunglasses all around your home and your car with worry, when they are on your head all along! But when you take a moment and tune into your sense of *feeling*, you notice they are on your head. Sometimes it is all in a breath! And this is one of the most powerful shifts you can make. We will speak on meditation for a moment, as this is a key concept, and meditation is a practice than can help you get out of the active thinking cycle so that you are more in tune with what is coming in, but standard meditation practices are not the only ways to do this—it is to find what works for you so that you can train your brain to stop searching and rather just let things float in. And in fact, this is how you access the cosmic source of all information, your inner knowing. The more you connect to your soul rather than your thoughts, you will find the answers.

And so some of you might find this connection through walking or nature or dancing or again, playing, or a standard meditation practice, but we will point out the obvious to you because it is so key. As you have seen meditation practices (and manifestation practices, for that matter) become more and more popular, these are trainings for you to learn to be back in your natural state—for meditation is simply connecting with yourself, allowing space for your Soul to come through, because it has been so clouded by "thoughts" that you have actively learned and are typically not fully your own, but based on conditioning. And through connecting to your soul, you connect to a new type of "thought" that many of you call a "download," which is the thought of the soul, the whisper of your soul. Why is it that so many solutions drop in when you practice meditation? You simply have made space, quieted any voices that are not your own, quieted the worry, and it comes to you. But we will remind you that this can be your natural state, as you always are, and is really how you are meant to be.

The same with manifestation, and you are taught your manifestation practices, but it is your natural state to manifest—you are alway manifesting, but why is it that you need "training" to realize how to magnetize what you truly want? What this is is a signal of how deep the conditioning goes, and what does it say about what is institutionalized when it has taken you so far from the state of where you can go with meditation, where it is something so difficult for so many of you to simply tune into the present moment, and yourselves—the most natural thing for you! Maybe this is where you let your children teach you a thing or two... truly!

It is important to recognize these things, and ask yourself what the blocks are to easily meditating, for the solutions to instantaneously and effortlessly drop in, for what you truly and purely desire to instantaneously come to you? These are all not only possible, but what you effortlessly do when you release all of the layers that have made you forget, and now is the time to remember.

part sixteen

From Want to Have

Much of your resistance to releasing the energy of "thinking" in the sense of searching, creating logic to go from A to B, for some reason is to think that you will lose this (you can hold onto any skill you want!), but also because you are in *fear* of being wrong! We ask you to reflect on all the times and ways that you have learned that it is "bad," or you would be reprimanded, if you are wrong—another deep level of conditioning that we send so much love to you to heal. For whatever leads you to feel as though you must live in fear to be safe is not in alignment with the Source of love, and is not in alignment with you. What are you afraid to be wrong about? What is it to be "wrong"? And this is where the resistance comes in releasing the labels of right or wrong, rather than simply is. And what about "facts"—well, here is the trigger of what you believe to be facts—are they really? For the perception could be different of what the "objective fact" is if it was seen in another way. This is where your society has promoted standardization of all, and again, through it, where there has been so much uniqueness lost.

Think of what the standard styles of clothing are, to even wear clothing, what you eat for different meals, when you eat, how you eat, what your homes look like, what a business should be like, the sequence of life events, and so on and so forth—these are all "shoulds." And even within your measuring system— think of it like a measuring cup. If you look from above, you think the perfect amount is measured, but if you get down to eye-level, you see you have gone over a bit. And then, more deeply, why is it "wrong" to make a mistake? What is a mistake? Again, what are your connotations of the word? We point this out for you to see the deep conditioning of the ideas of "right" and "wrong" in your society, and how deeply it goes, so you can start to unravel this for yourself, and thus unravel the fear—which is one of the heaviest weights to raising your frequency.

Again—you are not meant to live in fear! When you live in an energy of peace and compassion, the fear no longer controls you, as it doesn't have fuel to survive. And so, when it comes to "mistakes," you can see them as a clue, as a growth point, and a gift of where you can expand into new abilities, new information, new creation—and suddenly how you see mistakes is so much different! What would it feel like for you if you released the energy of "bad"—what if nothing was "bad"? And this is simply a thought experiment, but do you feel the freedom? This is the power of shifting your perception, and when you shift your perspective, you feel the associated shift in your energy, and in your body. And now there is so much more available to you, and what you want comes more quickly to you, as your focus is always on expansion, always on peace and joy, and that attention is what allows what you want to flow to you. It is in shifting your automatic state of being where you will find the biggest shifts in your life.

Many discuss thinking positively, and shifting what you're thinking, and this is all nice and well, but where it is limited is if it is always a process of "working" to make those shifts. The key is in making all of this automatic, so you transform from someone who keeps reminding themselves and has to work to shift their perception to see from the lens of love, to where that becomes what is deeply ingrained, and it is automatic to see everything from love. Again, effortless, there is no work, it is your flow to be in love, and it is your automatic way of being to *be* rather than always do, because you realize you are the creator and collaborator, and it will drop in for you. You will be guided. And all we require is your presence to it all, for it is always happening, and you trust the flow, and you are in enjoyment of and present in your life, rather than being in another moment.

Anywhere through this text you ask, "Does that mean it's bad to XYZ?" is where we will answer, that is the "wrong" question. This is where you are still attached to the labels of "good" and "bad." The invitation is to realize that, and instead ask, "When I am fully connected to my Soul, fully connected to love, what is it that is in alignment with that frequency—what

I do, how I perceive, and so on?" Notice where you still cling to someone else telling you what to do, what the rules are, the set instructions to "guarantee" a result—this is where you disempower yourself. It is all within you.

What if you were the one to make the rules, to set the instructions, to decide how to get there? We will tell you a secret—it is that when you have learned the way to achieve a certain thing, where you see the success is because you are so rooted in the belief it will work. Not to say the method itself does not work, but the level of belief is not to be forgotten. It is what you cannot *see* that is in fact more powerful, and the truth is that there are countless ways to achieve what you want. You block yourself if you feel that your way can't work, and again, we invite you to ask yourselves, what if you were writing the instructions?

You will see again and again, when people achieve in seemingly impossible ways—it is not that it was impossible, just uncommon. If you set a clear intention and let nothing sway you from achieving it, your energy and actions will shift along the path to always be in resonance with that way working out, and you get what you want, even if not always in the way you expect. This is where what you label determination, we might call intention, alignment, and energetic resilience. Imagine the energetic strength you would feel if you had clear, unwavering trust in yourself. A clear knowing that you can trust yourself, that you are a master co-creator and manifestor. How does that feel in your body? Take a moment, and soak it in. We will remind you—this is the truth! *You are!* And when you feel that elevated feeling, as if you are floating, almost where you might have before said it is "too good to be true," we counter with—this is your natural state! This is you coming home to yourself! This is where you are fully in resonance with your soul, and the fun truly begins, on a level greater than you could have imagined!

Where do you limit your happiness, your joy, your fun? Where is it that you might hold yourself back because you believe it must be counterbalanced with hardship? It is a different way of being for you to trust yourself and to allow yourself to be fully present in love *always*. And we ask you, if you had a billion dollars in front of you, gifted to you, would you allow yourself to receive it? If you had a full bank account that was replenished every time you spent from it, would you never spend?

Allow yourself to fully *be* in the unlimited source of love— it will not run out. Fuel yourself with it, for it will always be replenished. Fuel yourself so much that you are spilling over with more and more, and allow that love to fill not only you but to radiate out to others. This is how you influence so much in the field around you—and your physical reality shifts more and more rapidly. You will notice how the more you shift in your state of *being* in love, when your automatic state is in these higher vibrations, your physical reality shifts faster and faster. And while it takes longer for things to manifest in the physical than the energetic—one piece of this is trusting, knowing it will come.

When you order a handmade bracelet, you do not worry that it will be created and then delivered—it is coming. But you will notice that this gap gets smaller and smaller, and also that any gap is less noticeable because you are no longer *waiting around* for it to come to you, because you are so incredibly content and happy in the *now*, and this is the key to all. For we teach you how to call what you want into your reality in the physical, but we will say, this is the beginner's step, the beginner's lesson.

The higher you rise, the more you are in alignment with yourself, you start to realize that the whole process of getting there and how to get there does not actually matter at all, for you do not need to get anywhere. You might go places, explore, and enjoy, but it is not out of need, because everything you need is in the current moment. This will challenge your conditioning to push the goal posts further, to always look for another problem, and notice where you always see things to fix or complain about. How is this a reflection of an energy within you that can be released? A low-frequency energy looking to be fed…but you need not give it food.

part seventeen

Trust Your Magnetism

What is it that you feel you *need* to be happy, to be love? A partner? A different partner? A house? A move? A new job? Friends? Different friends? Time? Space? Your first step is to release the word "need"—you need nothing when you are everything. And you are everything, and now you remember this. You are an expression of everything, in your unique way, but you are energy—all energy made from the same, combined in different ways, and you have the ability to affect this energy. You are all. Never underestimate your power, dear one! And so, release the need, and be truly honest with yourself, coming from your Soul, about what you desire to feel—is it happiness? If so, feel the happiness in this moment, release the conditions, release the obstacles you put in front of yourself, and *feel*. Let it fill you up! Make a list of all the things that fill you up, and do them often. Laugh, play, smile, feel! And this is how you energize the power of your aura—you radiate this out. And from that feeling you will naturally be guided to your next steps.

Filled with love and happiness, perhaps you realize you need not make any shifts at all, for you have all you might need. Or you realize that with that happiness, you are ready to expand, and there is nothing to fear, and so you make choices that align you with different people, places, and opportunities. And you choose from that place of happiness, peace, and love, and check in with what is in alignment with your soul. And suddenly it is simple. When filled completely with love, gratitude, peace, and joy, you tune into what is in alignment with that frequency, what allows you to expand even higher— *what is in alignment with the purest, highest energy of my soul?* And you align yourself with those things, and allow the rest to drop away, creating space for what is in alignment to flow effortlessly to you, and you need not worry how or when—it is coming beautifully and perfectly, because you are radiating the frequency clearly, emitting the purest, clearest signal of your vibration, and so those that are in alignment will come to you, as they will see it. Trust your magnetism.

And what about those who are not in alignment with your frequency who are magnetized to you? This is where we tap into the fun of it, where we see the dance of frequencies and the power of free will, and the intricacies in the steps of expansion, growth, and exploration. For example, let's say you are emitting a pure, clear frequency of love and light, and somehow someone is attracted to you who is in anger and resentment. You might ask why this happens, and here is an example of how it will play out. We will remind you that everything is for you, and everything is also for them.

And so in this situation, they are attracted to you because there is a piece of their being that is ready to expand, and so it will look for a higher frequency around them that matches the happiness and love that does exist in them, and they will be brought to their opportunity to expand and be in a higher vibration. As they are around others in a higher vibration, they are able to raise their frequency, and so they are gifted this experience, but it is up to them to surrender to the process and allow the low vibrations to be released.

You, as a bright light, shine a clear signal, and they come directly to you, looking for more of that light—because their soul remembers that this is their true essence as well—love, and it is looking for more of that frequency so it can return to its natural state. For you, you might be offered a lesson, an insight, a realization of some of these energies within yourself, or an experience of low frequencies that allows you to realize again how good it feels to always be in happiness. And the more energetically resilient you are, the less that person with lower frequencies can "negatively" affect you.

And let's say this person tries to send low-frequency energy your way—through anger, perhaps. As a being of love, in happiness, in peace, you are in compassion, and the energy sent to you can be transmuted. When you are clear in who you are, you simply respond from that frequency, and all is well. As there are more of you who stand firm in your vibration of love, and continue to respond, the more the lower frequencies begin to be transmuted, for the fuel for low frequencies is more of the same. And part of your work is to continue to spread the love, to be in love, and to remind others that this is your natural state.

Again, we will remind you that this does not mean that you should not, will not, or cannot feel low-frequency emotions— for all simply is—it is not good or bad. All is part of the experience. However, you will notice that you start to respond differently, naturally. You might not respond to situations with these emotions when you might have before, for they might not resonate in your body, or when you feel them, you are able to transmute them more quickly than before—you fully feel them, release them when ready, and return to your highest vibrational state. It is like pressing down on a foam pad, noticing the dent, and watching it bounce back.

But these emotions are a gift in your human experience— powerful signs, powerful reminders, as expression is one of your most beautiful creations. We invite you to honor expression— self-expression, expression of others, but the key is always in intention. Why is it that you say what you say and do what you do? It is in the frequency of love, peace, and compassion for all that the intention stays in its highest, purest vibration, and you will notice the positive response within you. And a trigger from outside is when another feels the nonresonance in the vibration. It might "shock them" because they feel how powerful it is. And instead of noticing the opportunity for expansion, and where it is highlighting energies of a different frequency within themselves, they react and push away—this is how they stay where they are.

We will remind you, dear one, that you are not responsible for anyone else's growth. In fact, the more you focus on your own expansion, the more you take responsibility for your own energy, the more you stay aligned with authenticity, love, and your truth, when the foundational frequency of your actions and words is all of the highest love—this is how you best serve yourself and the world around you—as it is a reflection of you. And every moment you can approach with curiosity—*how can I expand here?* Everyone and every thing is your teacher.

Remember, the universe is supporting you in expansion, in remembering, in experiencing and learning that which your Soul chose—and you are able to work with the universe, and see it all flow together. What is real and what is not is up to you to decide—but how would you see life differently if you knew that all that was real was your perception?

part eighteen

Right, Wrong, and the Pedestal

Back to the topic of right versus wrong, we feel it is important to highlight where you are made to believe you are wrong, and where you might be unconsciously operating from the feeling that you are wrong, or need to be fixed. Instead of, "How do I make myself whole?" what about the question, "How can I remember my wholeness? How do I allow myself to be the wholeness that I am?"

Many of you spend your time looking for ways to no longer be "wrong," in the sense of what needs to be fixed, and the important distinction here is to ask yourself why you are in this exploration. Is it because you feel something needs to be fixed, or because you realize that you are whole and you are love and you wish to continue to expand and be simply *more* of what you already are—what you already have access to?

When coming from this intention, you will notice a difference in your results, as your energy will be quite different the whole way through—because you will be in wholeness the whole way along, and this is how it is magnetized to you so much more clearly.

Often you judge your feelings based on what is around you, and in a sense react to the circumstances, but what if you chose to instead choose your feelings and then see the world around you from that lens. And so, it is swapped. You do not need to be fixed. You are already whole, and everything else is more that you can expand into, and you can ask for more of that wholeness whenever you want—there is an unlimited supply of love. Why do you feel guilty or greedy asking for more? Here is another instance of operating from lack mindset, and this is not your truth, for it is one of the greatest illusions that there is not enough for all. There is enough, and you see this when you allow yourself to be in your highest state of being. There is always more, everything is energy, all energy can be transmuted, and so to believe that there is not more is to believe there is nothing, but in fact the truth is there is everything.

We will discuss the pedestal, a common "block" for many of you that is simple enough to remove. What do you put on a pedestal, in terms of life achievements, behaviors, attitudes, actions, emotions? Everything you hold on a pedestal is what you choose to place above you, and you are in so deciding separation, and placing yourself in the paradigm of "better than, worse than," one above the other, and it is like choosing to put someone in first, second, and third place when you could all be in first. When you are setting your intention and wishing to call something into your reality, is it because you believe it is better than where you are at now? Is it because you believe it is a better version of yourself?

And we will use this word casually, but we would like to make clear that "better" as you might have understood it generally is where you do not already see yourself as magnificent. This is where you start to understand that another does not have to fall in order for you to rise, that there is space for love and accomplishment and success and happiness for all, and that everywhere you label as "better" is where you block yourself from being in the curiosity, joy, and excitement of another's achievements, but also where you have decided that where you are at is not good enough, and suddenly you are not seeing yourself as the leader, the king, the queen, everything—for you are—you are magnificent! And so is your neighbor, your friend, your teacher, your student—there is magnificence in all.

But a society built upon the idea of "better than, worse than" has caused many of you to forget that you are whole, you are enough, you are love. You might have been told what you "have to do" to achieve "rank," in whatever that means to you, but notice where you take this as significance of better than or less than, as this is where you stay in 3D consciousness, which is not bad, but is where you are slower. And most of you are wishing to rise into a higher level of consciousness where it is not an effort or a pull to be constantly in a state of love and peace, but rather to flow through the world seeing it all this way.

And so, what does it mean to be in abundance? So many of you strive for manifestations of abundance, in whatever form—whether this is more money, more friends, more love, more homes, more opportunities—it is the energy of more, and that will manifest in the way that is in alignment with you. This is where we return to your multidimensionality, and as shifts are made in the higher frequencies, think of it as a computer game being reprogrammed. The video game is rebooted and then you *see* in 3D what the shifts were and how they manifest physically. And so, if you know that you want to feel abundant, all you have to do is be abundance, and this is where we return to how you are the universe.

As you move through your life and see the world, if you catch yourself making a judgment, ask yourself, *Is this my lens of abundance? Or is this my lens of hierarchy, not enough, needing more?* There is no need for judgment in the sense of valuing what is "better than" or "worse than" when you are fully in love and seeing the beauty in all. We challenge you to see the beauty in all—every being, every situation, and every opportunity, and notice how your world shifts. As you connect with higher dimensional beings who are here for your ultimate guidance, as you allow yourself to receive the support of the universe, and you feel the unconditional love, and how there is endless love, you notice that you are fully seen in your beauty, and how good does this feel? This is how you are meant to see yourself, and all others.

And you might ask, what of those who wrong you? What of those who hurt you? Where is the beauty in this? We remind you of this lovingly—your blocks to seeing the beauty are your emotional attachment. And this is where you zoom out for a moment, and if you saw the dance of frequencies in the universe, you would see that the universe was not punishing you, but rather was simply responding to all of the energetic signals being cast out—this is not only from you, but also from the many beings around you, in combination with choices made. We do not see things as coincidences, and we also do not see anything as what is deserved or not deserved. There is an understanding of vibrational match, opportunities for expansion, feeling contrast, challenges that present opportunities to step into higher versions of yourselves, soul contracts, free will, and so on.

For the same set of circumstances—you can say, "Everything bad always happens to me," just as easily as you can say, "Everything good always happens to me," just as easily as you can say, "Nothing happens to me," or "Everything happens to me." Or, "Everything happens for me." Or, "Everything neutral happens to me." Or, "Everything neutral happens for me." Or, "It simply is, and how do I expand from it?"

We would like to point out that your incarnation experience is like a speck of dust in the largest room you can imagine, what feels so big and vast and like a considerable length of time is simply a blip, and your soul knows the vastness of all that is, of all that you are. And if you zoomed out to a much higher place, the perspective would shift. If you took a single letter on the page and zoomed in 1000% you would see it one way, 150% another, 50% another, and 1% another, and the 100% compared to the 1% zoom perspective might be so different you would not even perceive it to be the same letter! And so it is to honor your perspective, and to realize that you can also shift it if you so please, and perhaps the perspective you have now will be helpful for a lesson, expansion point, or greater shift in perspective later on, and all builds on top of each other in beautiful, miraculous ways. And if you feel your vibration shift downward, through hardship or struggle, allow yourself to be launched upward in the other direction, in a way that allows you to experience the richness of the higher vibrations even more so. And so we turn to… appreciation.

part nineteen

Appreciation

Appreciation and gratitude seem to tie it all together, as these are some of the most powerful emotions for amplifying your magnetism. Think of a family member who gives you a gift. And you are laughing, screaming, crying, jumping with excitement over that gift. In response to that powerful vibration, in feeling the love and gratitude reflected back, the family member stores that energetic memory and wants more of that reflection, as it feels good for them, and gives you another gift, and the cycle keeps going, and so it is with the universe. Everywhere that you are in gratitude—true, deep gratitude—that signal is cast out, and where you are in appreciation is where more flows to you, as you fully soak in the energies that you receive with love. Where you receive and do not appreciate, there can be a type of energetic block, where you are not fully receiving.

This is similar to feeling emotions, and how so many of you say you feel an emotion yet you do not truly feel it. Saying you are sad does not mean you are feeling it in your body, and we invite you to come into your body and fully experience what it is capable of. When you are grateful, is it simply saying you are? Do the words inspire the feeling, or is it a feeling that inspires the words? Words can amplify and set intention, but the energy is much more powerful through emotion. A powerful emotion will do more than words, and will override the words. Words with emotion together are a force!

And so, when you feel gratitude, what would allow you to actually feel it in your body? Is it in your heart? Your stomach? Your hands? Your throat? Where do you feel it, and how do you feel? How can you allow it to fuel your body? There is always much to be grateful for—reading these words on the page, your hands, your eyes, your feet, your legs, the sky above you, love, laughter, imagination. There is so much right now with you! And it is one thing to acknowledge your gratitude, but another to feel it so deeply that perhaps you laugh or cry or dance or sing! If you are to say, "I have never felt gratitude that deeply," we invite you to practice taking time to appreciate what is around you, what it means, how much is available, and tune into your body. You can say the words that indicate gratitude to tell your brain to speak to your body, think about all that it means, and let yourself receive the energy, and eventually it will be the other way around. Where you are not fully able to receive is where you might feel blocked from the emotion of appreciation.

And so, how can you practice receiving? No ifs, ands, or buts! You can receive from yourself, but where can you receive from others? When you are blocked from receiving, there is an energetic imbalance of giving, and the universe is looking for harmony. When you are in the energy of receiving, what you ask for of the universe flows to you—think of it as opening the door for the manifestations to flow in, when it might be shut if you are busy "doing" inside. It is time to open the door, sit on the couch, and see what is brought your way!

But if you do not fully let yourself receive, you might not recognize that deep energetic feeling of appreciation, so pure, so much love—and often this is tied to illusions of unworthiness that many of you feel. Again, illusions that keep you in a lower vibration, lower states of consciousness, but now is the time to remember that you are of course worthy— this is your truth. There is nothing to do to become worthy, you already are. It is to let yourself be it. And the sooner you remember, the sooner you allow yourself to flow!

What are the blocks to receiving? You can say "thank you," and receive, and know that the giving will of course come back around to the giver, whether through you or another. And this is a key distinction, as we see things take place in the physical that are reflections of the energetic shifts that are made. These might happen through other beings, through situations, as the manifestation. And notice the magic when you see the work that is done through you, through others, and how you can all be such beautiful channels of love, magic, miracles, and opportunities. And the more you open yourselves up to receive, the more you clear your channels and allow yourself to be a pure channel of love, you will notice divine inspiration runs through you effortlessly, and Source is able to work through you effortlessly, in the highest frequencies.

As things are brought into the physical, what is the channel through which it comes? It is something of a vibrational match, of course, and you will see how high-frequency codes are coming through you as you maintain your authenticity as a high-frequency being. What a beautiful opportunity to be a channel for happiness, miracles, and love! And we remind you, you already are! But the message is clearer, stronger, and amplified the more you clear your vessel and raise its frequency. As you stay in authenticity, this work of love is performed through you, and through others. You give more than you realize. So often, many of you are out of balance with giving. And what judgments do you make of those who are in receiving? Is it that they are lazy? Selfish? Greedy? And why is this? And as you reflect on this, does it resonate as truth in your body?

part twenty

Discernment

And from here we move onto discernment—another crucial skill for mastery of your abilities in this form, and how to discern the frequency of something. And when calling things into your life, where you should move forward, perhaps where you wait, or perhaps where you release. The more you are in connection to your soul, the more you are filled up with and surrounded by the highest frequencies possible, the more you are able to tune into what is a match and what isn't. Once you stay stable in your frequency and have built the resilience to hold it, you will be able to pause a moment and reflect on what direction the misalignment is going in—higher or lower than your current vibration. Is it actually expansive, which sometimes is perceived as a "trigger," or is it leaving you with an aftertaste, a low feeling?

And when opportunities come your way, how do you feel? Is it just what you asked for? Remember, you are the co-creator, and you set your clear intention. And so, if it is exactly what you wanted, here we are! If it is a stepping stone to whatever you called in, here we are! You are on an exciting journey, and there is beauty and joy to be found in the process (a gift not to be overlooked!). And if it is almost what you wanted but not quite, here is a powerful moment of reflection—*what is my intuition saying? Is this something that could allow me to feel what I desire to feel, just in a way that I was not expecting?* If so, perhaps it has popped in, simply in a different form than you expected, and what a joyous miracle that can be! If it is close but not quite, and you honestly feel in your body it will not make you feel precisely how you wish to feel, but it is good enough, then it is your choice whether you say "yes" or not— there is no wrong or right. But recognize that it is your choice if you say "yes" to what is almost there but not quite.

However, if you say "yes" from an energy of worry or fear that you set your sights too high, this is from lack, and being disconnected from your power and intention. Remember that we are always in communication. The universe always communicates with you, and so if you are delivered your meal with the wrong side dish, you can gently say, "No thank you, this is not what I ordered," and we will bring out the dish again with the side dish you did choose. And this is one way that we communicate—it is close to what you want, but if it's not what you desired to create in the sense of not allowing you to feel what you desire to feel, and it is in your highest alignment to receive just what you want, then you can say, "No thank you," and we have gotten the signal that the energy was close but not just right.

And this is also where you can respond to the feedback we have given, in the form of an opportunity, by seeing if there is anywhere to adjust your own vibration to more purely reflect what you want, and from here you might notice pieces of resistance, fear, or scarcity energy running through, which you can transmute, and then notice how you receive exactly what you wanted before.

But to say "yes" to what was almost what you wanted but not exactly so is not to say you won't be happy, for many things can make you happy if you want! But it is to see that there is no right or wrong choice, but always more opportunities. And where you make decisions from a place of not wanting to miss out, this is an interesting thought. And really we invite you to tune more into the energy of exploration to experience more, rather than feeling you will miss out, because what is for you will not miss you—whether in this life or another.

With that, we also encourage you to think about where you might be closed off to opportunities, for sometimes we see you so headstrong that your vision is the vision, which is not to say is wrong, but that perhaps you overlook more opportunities for expansion, ways to see things in different ways. And perhaps you would have liked that as well—the same, more, or less. If you are walking a path to reach a home, you could perhaps take one road that happens to pass by a great field of flowers, bigger and more beautiful than you've ever seen before, or perhaps you take the other fork and go on the road where you see beautiful forest creatures and enjoy being amused by their activities. Options—there are options.

And if you take a certain road and perceive it to be the wrong one, why is this so? For you can always ask, "What if?"—but is this from wonder and curiosity, or feeling that you are in lack, missing out, and you feel that emptiness within you?

There is a process of learning to trust yourself, your flow, and when you trust yourself, there isn't truly a question of if it was the "right" choice, for that is not a wonder, but it simply was your choice, and what was presented as the path to be taken. And here in your perception is actually where you can shift the reality again. For perhaps you take the exact path you want, something unexpected pops up, and then you worry it was the wrong one, and the energy the universe feels shifts the next set of circumstances to be a reflection of that, rather than staying in the vibration of "this is for my highest" all the way along, and seeing how things line up.

If you are manifesting something specifically, you might notice distractions popping up on the road to achieving the end goal, and you send out signals to the universe along the way that will affect the goal. And this is where learning to hold your vibration makes you so powerfully magnetic, and you find that the "road" to getting there shortens and shortens until it is but a step or exactly where you are, because any distraction from your truest vibration shifts what pops up on the road in the path to get there.

When you notice doubt or fear popping up in others, how do you respond? Is this where you doubt yourself? This is yet another reflection of where you might be putting another's sense of discernment above your own, and why would another's be more important than your own? Yet again, a sign of the pedestal and hierarchy. What if this is your opportunity to be a point of expansion for this other—for if they ask you to question yourself, notice if this is from curiosity and willingness to grow, or perhaps a reflection of where they question themselves, amongst other possibilities. And where there are moments of pause, doubt, or reflection—what a gift! For these are always moments of strengthening your confidence and anchoring in your frequency, no matter what the outcome.

Perhaps you are invited to question your choices or opinions, and you reflect, and you come to the conclusion that perhaps you could see things from another light that is more expansive— what a gift! Or perhaps you question your opinions or choices, and upon reflection, true reflection, where you are open to change because you are in an energy of flexibility to allow for your greatest expansion, you reaffirm that your choices or opinions are in vibrational alignment with love and truth and compassion, and you get more confirmation of your direction, and how much is this also a gift!

There are many who mistake doubt or questioning that pops up as a "sign" that things are not "right" or they are not on the right path, and perhaps it is a signal for deeper evaluation, but the end answer can go either way. Again, notice where you are in fear or judgment, and thus fear can pop up, as well as the expectation that things will get in the way, and that there will be judgment. And we remind you—whatever your expectations are will be reflected in your reality whenever they are affecting your vibrational frequency. And so, this is where you can stand firm in your expectations. If someone disappoints you, do you give up on them? If so, what energy is that from? It is a great gift to hold firm in what you know people are able to achieve, for sometimes it is seeing that belief from another that encourages you to have it in yourself.

But the trick that you are learning, we hope, is that you need not have belief from another—it can come from yourself first. But this is how you can even more so empower those around you, for there is so much confidence to give, and what a gift to be confident in your abilities and your magic! Is this not what so many of you seek? Confidence, freedom, love—you will find that as you fully fill up on one, you feel the others come in as a byproduct, as you go higher and higher on the frequency scale, and pick up higher frequencies along the way! And so, when we say to stand firm in your expectations, here is another qualifier for you, which is—we mean clear intention, but where is expectation for you actually a box that could be limiting you? And so, it is to expect something, but also to be unattached—do you feel this is a contradiction?

Where your expectation overlaps with a hope, a want, is where it becomes muddled with energies of lack, and an underlying current of not already being a vibrational match. But when your expectation is firm in intention and confidence that you will receive what is perfectly in alignment for you, and openness to how it comes through, now your expectation allows you to see the world from the lens of your manifestation already coming to fruition, as a reflection of your knowing.

And this is key—being in knowing! When you know, this is also expecting, but it is different than expecting with a sense of wonder or waiting to see, but rather expecting with a knowing and confidence that it will arrive in the way that is in the highest and best.

And so, you've set your intention, you are already in the energy, what you have is already in existence, and it is being pulled down to you as you speak, and it will manifest in physical form. And there is nothing left for you to worry about, for it is not up to you to discover how or when. Allow the universe to provide for you, to work in its wondrous ways, and allow yourself to enjoy. But if you set an intention and are expecting something to go differently than described, that expectation is sent out as a vibrational signal, stronger than simply the sentence you say or write, because your emotion and consistent beliefs, which the universe understands energetically through their frequency, are the updated, stronger signals. And so then what you expect is being magnetized, and you see the world from the sense of that expectation. And so—what is it that you desire? And invite yourself to expect this to happen, and be in the joy of it!

This is where we feel the need to insert a brief reminder again that everything that allows you to be in your magic, the more you show the world your magic, the more you let yourself play and do what you love to do, what you are good at, whether or not it feels "productive," is your key to becoming more and more magnetic. And what you have been told is productive is really a very three-dimensional, limited view on productivity, and there is so much more to it than you think! For if your playfulness and your enjoyment is what allows your frequency to align with miracles dropping in for you instantaneously, is this not productive? Everything is productive! Rest is productive. Action is productive. Silence is productive. Speaking is productive. You are always productive. The question is, what do you want to produce? Align your energy and behaviors with what you want to produce, and it will drop in. But when you are so in the programming of always needing to do, thinking this is what leads to production, this is where you block yourselves from producing and creating all of the things that can be or must be produced or created through energies of being, which are perhaps your most powerful energies of aligning yourself with creation! It is how you *be*!

Remember that everything is a signal to the universe, you are always in communication, and so you can communicate through words, speaking or writing, you can communicate through action, you can communicate through belief, through visualizations—it is all a signal. So we invite you to send a clear signal. And this is where you might inquire, *Can you visualize yourself to the life you want?* This is one signal, and it is a strong signal that helps to work on your inner vibration and your beliefs, but that is not the only signal you can offer. It is also how you show up physically that sends the signal, and for some things the visualization might be everything, but are you feeling it in your body, and following through on the action?

The most important step is feeling how you wish to feel in your body—this is the most powerful signal, and carrying that consistently in your life. Being that vibration, then following with action in alignment with this. But if you are only sending out one type of signal, or a signal once, this is like expecting a lost boat to find the lighthouse when the light blips on and off for only a second, a single time, on a stormy night. How can you align every aspect of your life to be in accordance with what you want, and how you want to be?

Many believe that who they want to be is indicated by the physical—having certain things, being around certain people, perhaps living somewhere specific, but it is not things that bring you what you want—it is simply how you *be*—your authenticity, your alignment, your energy, your emotion. And so, if you are under the illusion that having all the things you see for yourself will make you who you want to be, this is backwards thinking. As you *are* the person, your physical reality adapts to you, as the energy around you dances and harmonizes with the signals you put out.

part twenty—one
Desire & Targeted Manifestation

And so, we will offer simple tools you can use when targeting things more specifically, but we invite you to remember that root-cause shifts, the overall vibrational shifts, the way you live in alignment, feeling your best and taking care of yourself, filling yourself up—this is the strong foundation for you to lay, so that anything else targeted comes quickly and effortlessly. Trying to target specific things without doing the underlying work is like trying to lose weight in one area of your body by focusing only on that area with exercise for one week before your big event.

More than offering you awareness around how manifestation works, we wish to empower you to step into your role as creator in your own life, and to realize all of the amazing things your life has to offer, the beautiful experience you are living, what a miracle to be in a physical form with a body that works so intelligently to always support you and to keep you in balance, to be amidst a world that runs by laws that even the greatest scientific minds of your time can hardly wrap their heads around. What a beautifully intricate, vast universe—you, an expression of energy in unique form! What an experience! We are so excited for you!

And so, we hope that your remembrance of your power empowers you to feel love always, and to notice an overall shift. And as you truly start to remember how manifestation works energetically, you might find that all the things you wanted to "target," the specific things you wished to call in, no longer matter as much, because you are in an ultimate, expansive state of complete happiness and fullness exactly where you are. And everything that drops in is a surprise gift from the universe that is better than what you could have imagined, but you didn't even have to set the intention for it—it simply flowed to you. And this is where you will truly see the magic of life, where you move past even needing to set an intention, for what would it be for?! All you could want or need is in you, and you are naturally attuned to being in curiosity and exploration, and so you naturally fall into opportunities and experiences that allow for your greatest expansion and growth. And you feel yourself in an endless sea of love and abundance and peace and happiness at all times, while simultaneously feeling it grow more and more powerfully, although you are unsure how it is even possibly so!

It is infinite, and growing. You understand now how what seems to contradict can coexist as both truths, because you are in abundance, in the Oneness, open to all expressions, and seeing how all energy can shift and move and how so much is in existence all at the same time, but in so many ways. This is your connection to the universe, as the Universe—something that you feel and know, but can't articulate. For it is the knowing, and the feeling, and the remembering that gives you all the information you need, and you are at peace with the limitations of words, as you see that vibration can encompass more than any words truly can. And you allow yourself to bask in the expansiveness of it all.

At this point we feel it is a good time to shift into some more specific, extra enhancement practices, we will call them, with any targeted manifestations, and then to go a bit deeper for those of you who are ready to explore even greater depths of this work.

If you ask yourself, *Is it wrong to want? Is it wrong to desire?* We wish to speak more to this, because we feel it comes up for many. Here is another example of where your brain is looking for examples of where you are wrong—and this is where you reprimand yourself, and all you need to do is shift into an energy of love. Notice the question again from that energy of love. And then, see how the questions themselves are living within the paradigm of wrong versus right, good versus bad. And the real question is—is this the paradigm that you do wish to live in and operate in? This is simply a choice.

As your world understands more about shifting consciousness, and raising it, it is easy to get into judgment. But realize what you decide is best for you is your opinion, and in fact, if you are to operate from a place of "no wrong or right" but then are claiming that that level of consciousness is better than, you are still operating within the lower levels of consciousness. You incarnated in this form at this time to experience it, to learn from it, to grow from it, and you can decide how you wish to see the world from here on out, and through this transmission we hope that you are able to make a choice more clearly, instead of making the choice based on the limited options that were placed in front of you.

It is to realize that when someone tells you you can choose this or that, you turn around and see there are infinite more options to choose from. And from here you can choose more clearly, in accordance with the vibration that you choose to be in, but also in knowing that you are a high-vibrational being. You are love, created from love, and it is your right to be in this state, to return to this knowing, if you so choose. And so, if you explore the question from neutrality, we invite you to feel into the question itself, and not try to logic your way to the "answer"— for there isn't a "right" answer from our point of view, but what is it that you feel around "wanting"?

Again, is the "want" from acknowledging it is not already a match? And how does this affect your ability to draw it into your now? Or are you curious if it is of a lower frequency to want in itself, and here we will share our perspective, and it comes back to the foundational frequency of it all—the "why" behind your intentions, your choices, your actions. Do not be afraid to ask for more, for what you want, but notice what the intention is behind it, because that is the fuel for your magnetism.

part twenty—two
Manifestation Enhancements

First we will begin with targeted attractions and some helpful enhancements. As you know the basics—clear intention, feel the energy, be the energy, and act from that energy—because you have what you want. You are the person that has it—you already feel it. Visualizations, as we have shared previously, and daydreams, are helpful enhancements, as are what you call affirmations or mantras. Speak out what you are, telling the universe, declaring it, and reminding your brain. And you can add to this by saying it out loud, writing it down, and repetition not from an energy of proving or convincing, but simply knowing and declaring.

Next, we will offer movement—dancing to upbeat music, jumping, giving your body physical signals of its excitement and happiness. Resting. Playing. Indulging in your childlike favorites. Indulging your senses and being present. Shifting your physical environment to be a reflection of who you truly are—this could be through what you wear, how you present yourself, your haircut, your furniture, your decor, your belongings, how you present your food. Charging your food with high frequencies so that your cells are fueled with high-vibrational energy. With your physical environment—creating symbols for yourself, representations of having what you want, or of frequencies. Perhaps a specific tea is a symbol for you of love, or comfort, or safety, or abundance, and as you sip this, not only can you charge the water with your frequency, but tell your brain and body and the universe that the tea itself is a symbol of this frequency.

You can do this with crystals, with a photo, with a stuffed animal, with any object that is a representation of the frequency you wish to fill yourself with. Perhaps a special coin is a symbol of abundance, and you keep it in your environment to remind you that this energy is always around you. Perhaps a particular blanket is your representation of safety, love, and support from the universe, and so every time you wrap it around you, you physically affirm these energies are with you.

Scents are a powerful way to magnetize what you want, and quite underused! You can utilize natural scents to represent specific frequencies, and this is powerful because the scent will harmonize to the frequency as a helpful bridge from the unseen energy into a 3D sense that is clear for most, before it is more physically seen. And you can use natural scents like peppermint, ginger, forest, roses, ocean water, orange, and so on. Attach that specific scent to your intention, and breathe in that scent every day—even better while visualizing and feeling. And this is how you get your entire body involved in being in the energy—feeling it in your now—and there you are! For example, if you link peppermint to abundance, every time you smell peppermint, your brain and body activate to abundance, and now you have a helpful trigger for feeling the energy.

You can use a similar technique with sounds—perhaps it is a specific sound you hear, or a song that is uplifting. And by utilizing sounds at the frequency that matches your intention, you can use sound as another way to link your intention, brain, and body, and to raise your vibration.

Next we will offer—physical links to gratitude. Again, you send out a powerful signal when you feel appreciation deeply in your body, and you can amplify this by treating things around you with gratitude and respect. Where you care for your money, with an organized wallet and bank account, where you care for your kitchen, keeping it clean, where you take care for your clothes, and your overall body—this is a sign of gratitude and appreciation, and thus the universe sends back more money, more sustenance, more health, and so on—as physical care is a sign of "thank you, more please," and the universe will deliver more of what is cared for and protected, from an energy of love!

Lastly, never forget the power of your emotions, and the intense energy they send out. There is a reason why you can palpably feel emotions in a room if you are aware. It is a much stronger energetic signal all around. And so, any time you are targeting, focus on filling your body with the emotion, and pairing the intention with that high-frequency emotion felt in your body. Physically feel the excitement around it coming through, for it is. Feel the excitement around having it, and being it, because you do and you are. Happiness, love, excitement. And you can utilize activities or memories to bring up these emotions as well, if this helps you to feel them in your body. Perhaps you utilize a powerful, happy memory to pair with your intention and your visualization. Perhaps you dance around excitedly while declaring your intention to the universe. Perhaps you watch a video that makes you laugh so hard you cry from enjoyment, and you pair this with your intention and your knowing.

There are endless tools available to you, and it is important to remember to have fun with it! Notice where you are getting too serious, for we have found that the frequency of your planet overall, for a long time, was in so much seriousness, and kept there by judgments of what is respectable, professional, and so on. And who is to say that another's standards are to be followed (especially when you tune into the intention around setting them)? Enjoy this experience, and you will see even more flow to you. Simply put, don't you notice that you are naturally drawn to happy people? This is a simple example of magnetism, and it is true of energy in many forms.

Fill yourself up with love and enjoyment, feel high-frequency emotions so strongly in your body, emit them out clearly, do not dull your shine, be clear with yourself and your energy, align yourself with what you are calling in, and it is here. And so it is.

part twenty—three

When Hardship Comes

Now we will move onto questions that may be arising, and diving into some deeper nuances and insights surrounding manifestation, attraction, and your natural gifts.

To start off, we are tuning into the energies of...

Can it really be that simple? This is where the doubt pops up around being in a state of happiness and flow, allowing your life to be in accordance with what feels good, with you staying in your highest vibration, and, can things fall in quickly and easily?

Well, if you believe they are not meant to, then they will be delivered to you in difficult ways, and if that is what you desire, then so it is, and this is up to you! However, yes, it can be much simpler than you think. This is part of the puzzle of life, and where have you been trained to believe something that allows for more ease is a shortcut, a cheat, a trick? You see how this has been taught in many ways, to make one question if it is too easy, because of the deep conditioning that it must be hard. We can assure you, it need not be.

The universe works in flow—as energies dance and harmonize —energy is looking for harmony, vibrational resonance. And so, the flow is the natural state of things. Where things slow down is where resistance is added, and so if you would like for things to be more of a puzzle than they need to be, then this is your choice! If you notice people who seem to have so many things simply drop into their lap—let this be evidence for you that this is available to you as well! And while it might not be what you think is common, it does not mean it is impossible or not how things are naturally aligned. The more of you that live in truth, the more you will notice what is common will make a 180° shift!

If things were simpler, what else would this give you time for? Space for? How do you keep yourself busy through making things more complex? Where does the challenge and the struggle make you feel like you are working, and you associate working with productivity and moving forward, but what if you could simply jump to the next, without the pushing or the pulling or the heaviness of it all? It is available to you.

We will remind you that the universe does not trick you. There have been many misconceptions planted that the universe tricks or punishes you, and this puts you in fear. The universe is in support of you and responds to your vibration— this is not associated with deserving anything, or punishing you for anything, it is simply the energetic dance. And the high-frequency beings, expressions of the One that are without solid form and filled only with love, without conditions to this love, are always guiding. And if you feel thoughts or energies coming through that do not feel like the energy of love, this is where you can clear the energy, transmute the energy, beam out light and love so strongly that no low-frequency energies can be in your field.

And this is where you need not put any entity on a pedestal, but rather practice your own process of discernment—you are the powerful one! And so, bring yourself into what you decide you want your "neutral" to be, in the sense of your comparison point. (We recommend love.) And then compare the frequency to that, and that is how you discern. And perhaps there are pieces of this transmission you resonate with, and perhaps there are pieces you do not, and that is all and well—you need not take on anything that you do not feel is in alignment with your highest and best, or in resonance with your soul. Your choice is powerful.

As another point related to this question, what of the people in your life you perceive to be sabotaging you, making things more difficult? Well, how can you shift the energy and learn the lesson? Any challenge, any butting of frequencies, anywhere you feel pulled down, is in fact where you can become so much stronger. It can catapult you into the next step, the next level. And so, perhaps you learn a valuable lesson that prepares you for what is next, perhaps you realize it is time to release that energy from your life, and this is protecting you from other circumstances, perhaps you become aware of a stored emotion in your body that is ready to be felt and released, perhaps there is something reflected back to you that is crucial for your next level of expansion. It is a choice if you make the situation about them, if you give away your power by staying rooted in an energy that someone is "doing something to you," that you are at the mercy of another's decisions. Free will is honored—this is part of the experience, but this is true for you just as much as the other. Your response can be empowered, or you can give in to the lower frequencies. Remember who you are.

Related to this, what of the question—why do bad things happen to good people? Again, we invite you to recognize that this is again coming from the paradigm of "bad" and "good"—and to label certain people "bad" and certain people "good" is generally a blanket statement of that person's frequencies, and if you looked further, you would see that there are low and high frequencies in everyone, and perhaps some are more imbalanced than others, leaning more in one direction than another, but we ask you to honor the complexity of humans themselves, and in what they choose to act on. We will also remind you that energy can be transmuted—this is not to say everyone chooses to, but it is to realize how frequencies can shift, from moment to moment and throughout a lifetime. And so, the universe does not label people as "good" or "bad"—and if you choose to, this is your choice.

We will clarify the question. If you are really asking, why is it that hardship comes upon people who are kind and loving, then you can get closer to an understanding. We will begin with the first part, which is—what do you mean by hardship?

For again, if you label hardship "bad," this is your choice, but what if hardship is a gift? And if this upsets you, this is where there is emotional attachment, which is valid for you to have, but we invite you to have recognition. There are lessons to be learnt, trials to overcome, that allow for the next level of expansion, and sometimes a person's energy is mixed in with an energetic dance of another's, and it is a question of which energies are more potent.

What we wish to clarify is that not everything that occurs is of your conscious intention, and this is part of the mystery of life, the journey, but it is a physical manifestation that will interact with your frequency in some way that is in alignment with the next part of your journey. And so, what might feel sad and painful in the moment could be the thing that builds strength, resilience, and determination, and what if this is what your Soul was calling for?

The most powerful lessons are typically learned in memorable ways, and in ways that offer you the gift of more expansion, feeling and experiencing love more deeply than you might have before, guiding you to opportunities that are in alignment with your soul purpose, if perhaps you weren't going off path, but energetically asking for support to get on track with a particular timeline.

And then for the second part of the question—we will address loving people—for there are many possibilities here, depending on the situation. People can be loving and kind, but also have energies such as fear, sadness, or anger stored in their bodies, whether or not they or those around them are fully aware of it. This does not make them "bad" people—it is part of their human experience. Someone can be loving and kind, and ready for their next level of expansion, and unless you are in their experience you might not know what it is their soul is calling for—what they are energetically asking for more of in their life. And if this is more love, for example, sometimes it is what we perceive to be the breaking of the heart that allows it to rebuild and repair and experience even more love afterward, to give you an example of how sometimes we are given gifts in ways that might be perceived as the exact opposite, although it might be difficult to understand in the moment. The universe is listening.

When one finds themself in the dark, the deepest depths of the dark, this also allows them to expand into the highest of the light. You understand this in your classical physics, as every force has an equal and opposite reaction, and so you can relate this to feeling the spectrum of emotions and experiences in your life. As someone goes into the depth of the dark and feels this, they can and will (if they allow) catapult into the highest of frequencies—and this is the gift of contrast. This is part of the experience you signed up for when your Soul chose to be here. This is part of your journey, and you can be in resistance to it, in judgment of it, or you can learn to dance with your Soul, to nurture your Soul, to love your Soul, and to go with the flow, even if the waters start to get muddy and unclear, but you can ride the wave, feel the crash, and let yourself move through it, reconfirming your power and strength, learning so much more about yourself than you might otherwise.

This is not, in fact, a process of learning to trust something that is outside of you, but rather the process of remembering that you can always trust yourself. It is your Highest Self that is guiding you to the lessons and the experiences that will allow you to unlock your next level of mastery, allow you to master this human experience, lead you to the doorways that you seek, lead you to the answers you seek, the purpose you seek— it is all your Higher Self guiding you. And it is to remember this that can allow you to release any resistance related to the question, "How can I trust what is outside of me?"

This is in fact the opposite of what we hope for you, for we wish to empower you with the understanding that the answers, the way, the creation, all, in fact, lies with you. It is to remember that your Higher Self is guiding you, your Higher Self embodied in this lifetime, with more "perspective" on it all, your Higher Self as an expression of the universe itself— you are everything.

This is to remind you of your power, to remind you of the vastness of the world but also how it is all one, making it all make sense again. This is your gift, this part of how you step into mastery, to understand what is a function of your beliefs, that you chose to be here to not know everything ahead of time, but to be in the enjoyment of the game. Have you ever played a game, or watched a movie, and thought, "I miss the first time I engaged with that experience"—for the first time is when you feel the emotion most deeply, you haven't yet "figured it out," and you're not sure what is coming next, and this is part of the excitement of it all. Your favorite book series—how you might wish that it was your first time reading it!

And so this is what is available to you in this lifetime, this expression, while your Higher Self, the larger aspects of your soul, might have already read the book, and while you can access the book, part of the fun of it, and why you (while you might not remember it) chose this experience was to be in the energy of the "firstness"—the creation of it. All the chapters might be written, but which do you choose to include? How do you mix and match the different storylines?

And so, you might have played a board game many times, and over time you have figured it out, and every time you play it is a slightly different experience. This is part of the gift you have now as well, being able to create the outcomes as you go, and to experience the "newness," even though you have played this game before. And with this comparison, we are initiating and unlocking the knowing, the memory, within you.

But when you get so attached to needing to know how or when or who, you are taking much of the fun out of it all! Do you trust your Higher Self to have created the optimal game—exactly what you might desire? Do you trust yourself to throw you a surprise birthday party, so to speak? It is really in coming back to yourself, which we will continue to instill, for far too much rhetoric and energy has been spent by so many of you on everyone around you, and while relationship is an important part of your experience, it is not to be to the exclusion of your relationship with yourself.

And when you are the creator, when you have so much power over your reality, why would you not deepen the relationship with the creator of your reality?! This is, for many reasons, the most important relationship of all. The more you understand yourself, the more you are truly in awareness of your Soul's desires, you will find that you are naturally led down the path of the most ease and grace and flow. The more "disconnected" you are to yourself, it is like having a master teacher in your house your whole life and never speaking to them. It is like becoming frustrated with the video game when you've never picked up the controller that sits right in front of you. The keys lie within, and what an exciting journey to discover the many aspects of yourself!

part twenty-four
The Rules of the Game

And you will notice the more you focus on yourself, your own vibration, how things make you feel, and what you feel called to, and the less space there is for the drama of others, the more you have compassion for others, but the more you are also attracting into your reality that which is a true reflection of who you are, and your highest frequency, and thus your reality changes. But can you take responsibility for what is being called into your reality and how you are responding? What is it that you can learn from everything around you? Here lies the next piece of the code to unlock—what if you were to have more rule over your reality than you think?

We invite you to reflect on how much of "the way it must go" in your world, in your reality, is based on the rules of what is around you that were imposed on you or told to you, for much of your expectations have been created by what you have been told they should be, and now we are to make this conscious. If you have been told that it is normal to sacrifice your own needs for another's, you will take that on as a "rule" of your reality. If you are told that success requires intense willpower, difficult work, and disregarding your heart, then these are your expectations.

But what if you were to write new rules to your reality? Perhaps that all around, you are meant to be happy, joyful, aligned with your purpose, and bonding over creation and happiness—and anything else is a sign of misalignment. Perhaps, that the norm is to live as close to nature, to your natural state, as possible, and the opposite is confusion. Perhaps, that you need only ask to receive a miracle, and that miracles happen every day. Perhaps, that you are always supported by your Higher Self, energies in the Higher realms that are always looking out for you, and that everything is happening perfectly for you. Perhaps, that any jealousy that comes up is not in fact jealousy but an indication of a desire, and it is being placed in your reality so that you are aware you can ask for it and receive it. That your world is a reflection of what is inside, and all you have to do is stay in alignment with your soul, remember your truth, and all else falls into place in accordance with this. Perhaps, that everyone around you is here to support you and teach you one thing or another, and you expect all interactions to go harmoniously. Perhaps, that you are inherently worthy, and any time you feel otherwise, anytime you feel doubt or fear, this is not from your truest self as an expression of the One, love, but rather a signal that something else is off, and you are able to feel compassion for what is around you, or there is an opportunity to step into a higher version of yourself.

What a beautiful signal—every time the fear or the doubt pops up, this is your sign—you have a doorway in front of you to step into your next level of growth, mastery, and ascension through this human experience, and so many of you are ready to go beyond what you have been taught. So many of you have been feeling for some time that what has been "standardized" is not your truth, and so now is your opportunity to write your own rules to the game, to this reality, that are in alignment with your truth. For when you try to live in a reality where you are told things must be in a way that is not in resonance with your soul, you will constantly feel off, and perhaps you perceive you are wrong or not good enough, and none of this is your truth.

Dear one, you are love! This is you coming home to yourself! This is you coming home to yourself as a creator of miracles, if you let yourself be! For we wish to send you miracles, to support you, but we are not to override your free will, and so it is to realize how powerful that is—to have free will, to feel the depths of your emotions, to have divine guidance and protection all around you, to have access to your Higher Self at all times—to realize that you are an expression of the One—this is *you*. It is to start to become aware of the signals within you that are not in alignment with your truth as an expression of the One, and to remember the messages, signals, and feelings that are. And so where the voice might have been quieter, it will become louder if you let it. It takes compassion for yourself, love for yourself, and this is your natural state. Are you ready to return to your natural state?

Where are you in hiding? Where are you hiding aspects of your truth from others, from the world? Where are you hiding your gifts? Your gifts were perfectly designed, perfectly chosen for this experience, and you have them for a reason. You have the keys, the codes, to unlock happiness for all, other expressions of you, but where you, and all around, will feel off is when you are not utilizing your unique gifts—which come naturally as a byproduct of you being you. And so it is to peel back the layers of everywhere that you are not truly being yourself, and for some of you this might feel obvious, for others it is more subtle. It is when you say things that are not *you*, but the common language, it is when you follow the trends because you are hoping it will make you feel accepted—but this is simply a reflection of where you are not accepting yourself! It is time to not only accept yourself, but to *love* yourself. When you are in full acceptance, there is no room for resistance, and when there is no room for resistance, you drop the blocks that could be in the way of you magnetizing exactly what you desire.

And what if the manifestation doesn't come through? Trust the timing, trust the how, trust the higher version of yourself. It is happening if it is for you, and if it does not come to you, it is for your protection. And so, can you let your ego step aside for a moment and again, trust the higher aspects of yourself, trust the universe? For if it is not in your journey, if it is not meant for you, this is out of love, and so you will not receive it. Ask and you shall receive if it is available for you in this expression—while that timeline might be different than what you expect, and if you do not receive it, you are receiving something greater. It might be a different version of the original intention, or it might not be that intention at all, but rather what you really were looking for—and what is it that you are really looking for—satisfaction? Love? Feeling successful?

And you will run in circles believing that these come from outside of you, for they are sourced within you, and when you are embodying love, it is expressed in your environment. And where you push or force something to happen, it is important to note what the frequency is underneath the request. Are you hungry for power? Greedy? Lacking trust? Feeling unworthy? And so, what is it you hope to call in from that frequency?

And this is not a warning but rather an explanation, for you will learn this lesson many times in your life. You already have, but so many of you don't have the awareness of the lesson itself, and so it does not truly feel learned. And when you think you already know, the question is, but has it really integrated? Have you embodied the knowing? Allow the knowing, the feeling, the lesson to sink into your cells, and when it has, you will show up differently. To race through life is to miss out on so many of the most transformational lessons, and these are lessons that you learn again and again, but we repeat, you don't truly *learn* until it has integrated, and the behavior or pattern has shifted, or you are communicating with the world around you in a new way, for this is the signal to the energies around you that your frequency has truly shifted, and now you can move to your next lesson of mastery.

But if integration of the lesson hasn't occurred, then the energetic shift will not occur within you, and so aspects of that energy that still reside in you will continue to attract in that lesson again, perhaps in a different way. The universe gets your attention in many ways. *You* get your attention in many ways. When reminders come in through the universe, we remind you, this is you getting your own attention, but just through an external expression rather than internal, and so the Higher aspects of you see what you pay attention to and what you don't. So many of you say you know, say you have learned, but you do not take action in accordance with what you say is a "knowing," and so, it is not truly a knowing.

There are times in your life when something is shared with you in a certain way, you see something in a certain way, you experience it, and while you might have before, this time it is profound, and you feel your world shift, and your energy shifts. This is the *knowing*. When you are able to say, "Ah! *I see now!*" And from this you can start to see what it means to really *see*, and understand the phrase, "do you see how..." itself—because seeing is rooted in knowing, not simply your third-dimensional vision. You are moving beyond this now. And even from a three-dimensional standpoint, what you see will depend on your awareness, your vibration, for how often do you drive a car and forget how you got there? How often do you walk by a small forest animal and not notice? It is all in what you are focused on, what you are open to receiving, what you are open to embodying. And so when you wish to learn more, when you wish to understand more, open yourself up to the awareness of it—this is the signal to the universe to send more your way.

part twenty-five
Focus on Your Truth

What you focus your awareness on expands. What you spend more time on expands. When you spend every day of your life doing a certain task, it becomes part of your life, and things develop from it. And when you are focused on what you do not want to occur, the energy that fills you is worry and anxiety, and you expand that out, and then what do you call in? And so you can decide that it is a thought, but not in alignment with your truth, for you as the creator. You as a divine being of light need not rest in worry, and so you let it go and say, "No thank you to that, but yes, please, to this." Perhaps let your daydreams guide you.

Where are you getting frustrated with yourself for being in sadness, frustration, or anger? Thinking about things that you do not want does not get you where you want to go. And we know many of you have heard this before, but you might feel caught in the cycle and ask, "But how do I get out?" Again, we return to—dropping the resistance. Showing acceptance. If you were to comfort a child, it is not to get angry at them for feeling fear, but rather to let them feel what they feel, show understanding, and then offer another way—and you see their eyes light up from this! The childlike wonder that brings us back to ourselves…for children are powerful creators, and there is much to learn from them—their souls so clearly shining out through them and around them!

Accept your thoughts, and send them love. By sending them love, you are able to transmute the fear, but the more you energize low-frequency thoughts with more low-frequency energy, the more you are intensifying the low-frequency energy, and so the cycle continues! Our advice is to drop the resistance, recognize the thoughts, feel into them, and learn from them. Let yourself feel. Be in curiosity—where did this come from? Remind yourself when this is not your truest essence of love, and so, what is it? Another's worry? An unconscious "rule" of your reality that has now been brought into awareness, and you can change? Ego attempting to keep you "safe" based on its own "understanding," but your Soul can see higher? Send it love. Send it so much love that it is transmuted. Create a new path, a new vision, a new "rule," and set the intention to anchor this in. Let it soak in. And if it comes up again, you can repeat the process. The repetition retrains your body—for it was conditioned in one way to begin with through repetition, and now it can be adjusted also through repetition, but this time you have more tools—you are aligned with truth.

Things can change in an instant if you allow them to, and if they are meant to (perhaps another new "rule for your reality" you might like to add, if it resonates with you), and when you have anchored in this knowing, then you will notice that habits, beliefs, and patterns all shift in your life much more quickly than those who are still playing by the limitations of "how it must be" which is really rooted in "how it's always been, as I've been taught in this lifetime." And we will also shine some light on this—what is common is different everywhere, another place where people can get caught in ego and believe that what is common in their aspect of reality is the same for all. This is deciding to stay in a limited perspective. But when you make the conscious choice to step out of a limited perspective and expand it outward, suddenly you see there are endless possibilities and then, what will you choose?

And the more you learn to sit with this, the more you will find you receive information, guidance, and manifestations more quickly, because what blocks so many of you is staying rooted, without realizing it, in a limited perception of the world. This is easier for your brains to understand so that they can make sense of reality, put it in compartments, group things together to start to learn rules and categories for faster processing, and so this has served you in ways, and there is also another way. You can expand that possibility field out, and all around you, into infinity. And instead of going into the filing index of what you have encountered, open yourself up to the vastness of the universe, and there you will find so many more possibilities that feel more in alignment than what you have been used to. And again, it has been helpful for your brain to guide you to a few options from so many that exist, but what if those few that feel aligned are based on a larger segment that are based on a reality that as a whole vibrates at a frequency different than what you desire?

Imagine going to a bookstore and letting yourself pick up four books to choose from—your intuition led you to those four, and this is a way that you are guided to what is in most alignment. But what if you realized that you were only looking on the first floor, and what if you did the same on the second floor of the bookstore? And so, say you chose another three books from the second floor that your intuition guided you to. But what if you took all seven books together—which would you choose? What if the first floor is nonfiction, and the second floor is fiction, and your soul was truly calling for fiction all along? And so if you stayed on the first floor, you could have chosen your favorite book of the first four, and perhaps had a great experience, but what if the experience that was in higher alignment for your soul was actually on the second floor? And when you allow yourself to finally go to the second floor, a piece of you feels full and aligned, in a way you never have before, because then you realize that the best, most aligned choice for you on the first floor in fact had less resonance for you than any options on the second floor. And with your book from the second floor, you feel aligned, you feel peaceful, it simply "clicks." And more, what if there was a book of even deeper resonance in an entirely different store? This is the value of expanding your perceptions and letting yourself choose possibilities that are beyond the realm of what you already "know."

This also allows you to step into a new level of creatorship. How do you manage infinite possibilities? This is a skill—a skill to know how to get more precise within infinite possibilities, but also to get more comfortable in the vastness of all that is. When you allow yourself to get more comfortable in the vastness, you build the energetic muscle of resisting your brain's desire to immediately try to process based on what it already knows. And when you can spend more time in the curiosity, the vastness of possibilities, you allow yourself the chance to choose something different, if you want, than the automatic processing, which might be rooted in an old perception, an old fear, a frequency that no longer resonates—and this is how you expand.

Your body is made of energy, and you are emitting an energetic field. And so, the key energetically is to transmute any frequencies in your body that are not in alignment with truth, to raise your frequency to be in alignment with your truth—love, joy, compassion, gratitude—and so the signal is clear, but then to project the field outward. And so, you can understand expansion in a number of ways, including expanding your frequency in the sense of raising it higher, but also radiating it out, projecting out your signal, and so— you become a stronger magnet. Imagine how quickly you can create, how deeply and purely you can feel love, how vibrant you can feel every day if you allow yourself to be the most powerful magnet that you are!

This process is all a shift within you. When you shift yourself, you shift how you see the world, you expand your ability to see what is available to you, and you expand what is available to you. But it all begins with you—that is how powerful you are, and this is what you are here to understand. This is your right. Many of you have had the experience of speaking to someone who just "doesn't see it." You might see in others where they are missing the mark, where they are complaining about their lives—but you can also see how they are playing into the situation, whether or not they mean to. And similarly, it is to see it in yourself—to remind yourself that you have more power than you think, because you have choice in every moment. You have decisions in every moment. And that choice might look like a visible action, but it might also be choosing a different perspective. It might be an energetic shift. It might be in the unseen.

And you will start to understand how working with the unseen is the most powerful way to shift your reality, and let it drop in. And here you see the magic in the world, but most do not see the magic in the world because they do not allow themselves to. Because they do not take responsibility. Because they choose to believe it cannot be for them. Because they do not ask for what they desire. Because they are not willing to align themselves with what they desire. Because they do not trust themselves. Because they are impatient. Because it is "more comfortable" to stay exactly where they are, even though they are not happy.

It is to learn to make the uncomfortable comfortable—here is one of the greatest shifts of all. To trust that you are always up for the challenge, for you would not be presented with the opportunity unless the universe was giving you a key to step into the next level of yourself. This is how you empower yourself—to remember that it is *you* who creates a shift in *your* world. Your world might not be the same as another's world—can you be at peace with this? Can you be at peace with another living the way they wish? This is their choice. And when it triggers you when another does not like their world, is sad in their world, but does nothing to shift it, they are your teacher. What can this teach you about yourself?

The Universe, your Higher Self, is always speaking to you.

part twenty-six
You Are Always Manifesting

We will remind you that you are manifesting at all times, and you will gain more conscious control over this process the more you integrate mindfulness into the way you live. It is a helpful start to have dedicated time to focus on what you want, but the key to being a powerful magnet is to embody the knowing that you are always communicating with the universe, speaker phone is always on, and so you bring this mindfulness into your day.

For if you open a concentrated period of time for envisioning, feeling the feelings, setting intentions to create something, what about the rest of your day? Do you let yourself shift back to how it was before? It is a consistent energetic shift to be in alignment with the "new" you—and yes, it can happen at any moment. Can you give yourself permission to shift at any moment? If another can change overnight, why not you? Your present now can be different from your next present now—one second to the next, or what you perceive. And it is to remember that the notion of time is a construct for you, and so really you could say that the next second is just as significant as your New Year's Resolutions, as your birthday—the next second is as significant as who you are 10 years from now.

Lessons are typically learned over time, and so you might correlate a shift in energy with time, but we will invite you to release the idea that things *must* take time to change. Sometimes, they do take time, but this is different than to believe they must. In that belief, you are already limiting what is possible for you. When they take more "time," it is to know this is for your highest process of learning, but you can speed the process up the more you truly learn the lessons, the faster you embody a higher vibration, and so on. And so when you become used to changing quickly—internally, not externally—(and remember, the energies around you respond to the truth of vibration, not simply what you "want" to project) you will notice that things come to you more and more quickly, and you become a faster manifestor.

Here, again, is the dance between free will, control over your reality, and also your higher aspect which is still you, another version of you—the universe, creating exactly what is in alignment for you. You are co-creating, each playing your part, and like any beautiful partnership, this requires trust. How interesting it is that so many of you find it more difficult to trust yourselves than what is outside of you—especially when what is outside of you is in fact a reflection created by you. It all comes back to you!

Are you mindful of your constant communication with the universe? Or do you perceive it to only be at certain times? It might be intentional at certain times, but it goes far beyond this. Imagine having a pet who is with you most of the day, as you do your daily tasks, and at the end of the day the pet sits with you and you communicate with it. It would be silly to think that that concentrated time at the end of the day was the only time when the pet was aware of your energy, and so it is with the universe. Your Higher Self is always with you, in you—the universe is always with you, otherwise, you would not have a perception of existence. And so, the messages are always being sent.

Through this you can start to see your life as what it is—*fun*! Recall when you were a child and you played a game all day long—so it is now, you always have a walkie talkie with the Universe. So, what are you telling it all day long? Being in awareness all day long allows you to fully engage with that conversation. If lessons and opportunities were being shared all day long but you only focused on them for five minutes, your "progress" might be slower because you are not conscious of everything else being shared, even though it is available to you. When you are in awareness, in mindfulness, all day long, you are constantly "hearing" what the universe has to offer, and there are more opportunities for learning and integration, and you will notice your reality shifts much more quickly.

And you might ask, *Is everything significant?* In a way, yes, and in a way, no. It is to remember that you ascribe meaning to what is around you. So many of you are looking for meaning, and so you have this opportunity. But you can decide if you will give this life meaning or not, and this is your choice. What feels right for you? What fills you up? We will also point out that many who are looking for deeper meaning misdirect this energy to attracting in drama, because they have gotten used to untangling those energies and feeling the intensity of emotions to feel "meaning," but what if you could feel the intensity of high-vibrational emotions for your "meaning" instead? You can create meaning in different ways, and it is to be aware of when the meaning is created through low-frequency interactions—this is your choice, and it is to realize that it can be created in another way. We will add, the "creation" can simply be recognition of what already is. It is an energetic shift, an awareness, rather than anything new.

Your world is interesting—can you see this? For it is a reflection of you, the energies are always interacting with you, and you are seeing the laws of physics in your dimension play out at the same time as understanding laws of higher dimensions, and many of you might feel caught between the two. What if you have access to both, and let yourself explore how they play together? It is to understand that the laws of your dimension shift if you enter another. As you become more integrated and connected to higher parts of yourself, you will resonate more with laws of the universe than that which feels "smaller" to you, and you will realize how much more there is to science than what you have learned. And you might ask, "How much progress have we really made?"

Through this information, we feel the energy of "getting caught up" with it all and trying to understand it all, which is a common block for becoming a powerful magnet. Your soul knows things without knowing why, because it is in full trust. And often when you get "caught up" with understanding, you are deeply in what you feel makes sense logically, and you are operating by the old rules. There is a new way to be. There might be moments where you realize, "I am choosing what is safe to me based on my 3D experience rather than exploring what else my soul inherently knows," and this can offer you insight. The key is to be conscious of what you are choosing, and that is available to you—the choice.

Where do you block yourself by trying to understand it all, when understanding it all at once might not be what is for your best in this experience? We remind you—that was not what your soul signed up for in this embodiment. Your soul wanted the experience of learning as you went. To know it all at once would defeat the point, and then where is the wonder, the curiosity, the fun, the magic of it all?

Here lies another gift within your range of emotion— the wonder! The excitement! When you find yourself in excitement, in delight, in pleasure, let yourself radiate this out, let yourself deeply feel it, and ask for more, if you so desire! In this way, you communicate with the universe and ask it for more, and you can use the power of this frequency that you are feeling in response to something to remind yourself of what it is to be in your natural state.

When something elicits delight or joy, let the vibration soak in, and realize that you do not actually require something outside of yourself to create that frequency. It is to remind you who you really are. And there you are in these energies, asking for more, the universe says "yes" to this, you attract more of this to you, and you create more wonder in your life. What a blessing to live a life that is filled with wonder and excitement! And you can create this when you simply decide, and let yourself build the momentum, and keep up with the momentum.

And so we will ask you, what is the momentum currently headed toward in your life? What are you focused on? What are you continuing to push forward? Is it love? Worry? Fear? Doubt? Anger? Insecurity? Play? Freedom? You can shift the momentum if you desire, but you must first realize where the momentum is headed if you are to do so. And this again requires the responsibility of asking, "What am I energizing?" With momentum—you might perceive this to be a very physical thing, and the physical is a part of it. What are you spending time on and taking action on? Who are you spending time with? What direction is it headed? What is it for?

If you are in unhappiness, if you do not enjoy your career, if you are looking for deeper friendships, and to get healthier— how are you adding more momentum to that continuing to be your reality? This requires honesty with yourself. There is, more importantly, the nonphysical—what is your energy emitting? These are the thoughts about and to yourself, what is unconscious, what is stored in your energy body, the nonverbal communication that makes up most of the communication with the physical and nonphysical beings and energies around you. What is your subconscious magnetizing? These are the programs underneath that are to be brought to light, and from doing this you will notice a shift.

It is all in awareness. From awareness, you can shift your energy. This is in observation. Where do you float through life unaware? So many go through their lives simply following whatever trajectory they find themselves on, they let the momentum take them, and they say they want something different but they're not even aware of where the momentum is taking them. The key is for *you* to be the master of your life, rather than to allow life to master you. It is for you to take control, to see what is there, and there you find empowerment. Empowerment is always available to you.

It is to think about who you are spending time with, how it makes you feel, how you spend your free time and why, how it makes you feel, what lights you up, what keeps you neutral, what brings you down, how you feel in your body, what energies are around you—it is to see what affects you! And everywhere that resistance pops up and you say, "I can't"—this is your sign that you are disempowering yourself, living in an illusion of "no choice," when here is your opportunity to be creative! True creators are creative—and so, allow yourself to create something you haven't felt before.

part twenty—seven
Confidence & Judgment

We will speak on confidence more here, because confidence and belief are so intertwined. If you lack confidence in yourself, you also lack belief in yourself, and if you don't believe in yourself, then you are disconnected from yourself as the creator, and how do you expect to make the shift? If you do not have belief in yourself, this is to not have belief in anything at all, for everything you perceive is in fact coming from you. You might ask, but how do I build my confidence? This is to come back to your truth. To bring it into awareness. And to make choices that resonate with your soul. When you lack confidence, you are staying in a disempowered state, and often waiting for something outside of yourself to pull you out of this.

You might find inspiration outside of you, but to empower yourself is a choice. You can decide that confidence is something you have to work for, or you can decide confidence is innate. You can decide to create confidence every day through your choices. What around you inspires you? What drags you down? All of this is feedback. It is not the truth of your soul to lack confidence—this is where you are in illusion. And when you have that awareness, you can recognize that lack of confidence as not true, and so it can be released. In simply receiving this information you are returning to this knowing, building confidence throughout.

The resonance with the word "confidence" will be when this fully integrates, and you will know when it does. It can be in an instant, or it can be over time. It will integrate that you have control. That you can define what gives you confidence and what does not. And if you have already decided that it is external validation, then you have already decided that the rules of your reality make it harder than it needs to be to feel fulfilled, and that is your choice. That is how powerful you are. But those who are in confidence are simply aligned with their truth, in flow with their soul, know who they are, and have realized that they are the creator of their own confidence— that they *are* confidence—for there is nothing more worth believing in than yourself.

All that you perceive around you is from you—you "are" the "technology"—you can master your life, master your energy. Your soul is vast and wise and infinite, and when you drop all resistance to yourself, you come back home to that knowing. In this effortless confidence, you drop resistance to following your soul's desires, you return to alignment, and you make choices that are for *your* best, not what you perceive to be for anyone else's. That is not for you to worry about (as they are actually one and the same—following your alignment supports that for others). And with all of this is releasing resistance to yourself, and as we have discussed, it is this resistance that puts up energetic blocks to you powerfully magnetizing more of what you want.

We remind you to ask yourself, "What do I get to release so that I effortlessly emit a clear signal of what is me, to attract what is for me?" And so, you understand that in a world that you might feel bogs you down, that is the fun of it—to realize they are all illusions, all different levels of your game, and when you remember that you are the strong one, the powerful one, and you are the main character, you rewrite the code, be the designer, and take on all the roles. We are waiting for you. Are you letting your life pass you by, or are you being the main character? Are you being the writer? Are you at the mercy of the script, or do you remember that you can change the lines whenever you want? This is the remembrance. This is the knowing. This is always available to you—and here you find flow.

What we are coming to is how you add power to your manifestation, to what you are calling in, and how you work with the flow. First, it is to let yourself be in the flow, and to follow your desires, for this is working with and from your Higher Self, as life is allowed to flow through you, and any obstacles or challenges meant for you to teach you the lessons for your next level of mastery will certainly find you. You need not create them for yourself as so many of you try to. Amplify out the signal of what you desire. And if this is in alignment with your soul, your lessons, your contracts, and truly with your Highest Self, you'll see how quickly it can come to you. How can you be clear with the universe?

Most importantly, it is through your energy and your belief—what you believe is possible, and shifting a hope to a knowing. It is through asking, and taking action in alignment with receiving, making choices that amplify the signal. It is through embodying the one who already has it, for you know it is yours. It is in your words. But it all begins with your energy, within you, and from this the action, the language—it all comes from embodiment. It is the openness to receiving. It is being available for support. The truth is that the universe is always supporting you, your Higher Self is always guiding you, but are you in resistance or not?

Again, we invite you to drop your resistance, and see what flows to you. And we will remind you that this is true as well with things coming into your reality that perhaps you do not like, and also of things coming into someone's reality who you perceive to not be at a high frequency. Beyond the discussion of judgment, but feeling into their vibration—it is quite simple—what is a vibrational match will come to them, and there is more than meets the eye when you are observing what other people "receive" and the quality of what they receive. It is key to allow each individual to be on their own path, and where you do, the more you will feel this come back to you as well.

But the universe does not judge if it "likes" someone or not, as all are expressions of Source, as much as this might create tension in you to think of this. But it is to realize that all communication is through energy, and your perception, likes, or dislikes are your own, based on vibrational resonance combined with perception of it, and the universe is simply responding to and dancing with what another puts out. And so the person who says something you perceive to be "rude" or "mean" but has a strong sense of self-love, self-worth, confidence, and clarity in signal will receive what is a vibrational match to them.

What is underneath the question of, "Why do mean people sometimes get good things?" This is often a judgment of yourself, a comparison, a worry about someone else's reality or experience as a way to deflect exploring your own, and also a feeling of "it's not fair," and this is where you are not in trust with yourself, who is choosing and creating this experience—perfectly designed for you, although you might not always feel it in the moment. Your beautifully complex life, the journeys you take, the trials and overcoming—these all make you who you are.

And the energies around you respond to the totality of vibration, the beliefs that someone has decided are their rules of reality—and you always have the same opportunity as any other to shift beliefs for yourself! It is also to remind you that a moment of being in low-frequency energy does not condemn you to a lifetime of attracting in just that—there is room for shifting and growth, while not everyone might take it, and while you might have been made to believe it is not so. We invite you to ponder how this creates fear in people—to believe there is no room for what you perceive to be "mistakes." For when this is your belief, you feel chained to the beliefs of others of what is "right" and "wrong"—and this is all an illusion through the power of the mind. You can release yourself and take your power back when you realize what the illusion was all along.

part twenty—eight
Group Manifestation

We will also explore the dynamics of "group manifestation," as you might say—how does it work when others are calling something in with you? And we will go a step further to offer a perspective—we are open to practices for manifestation, there is no judgment of right and wrong, but we wish through this text to offer you a way of constantly being in your knowing that you are always manifesting. And so it is simply how you *be* that calls things into your life without effort or focus necessarily, but just to receive the reflection back of the power and the magic of your own energy—for you are that beautiful, that much love, and you receive it back to you.

We will return to the idea of group manifestation, and this is where there is so much available to you as a whole. Through the illusions of division, groups of people can stay stuck when they are all caught in low-frequency beliefs together—told they are not good enough, don't know enough, told they are wrong, and also left confused, and we will invite you to think about how this shows up in your society. When you are operating from the belief that nothing is ever enough, that you are always wrong, always needing to prove yourself, you are kept on a hamster wheel, and yes—it is time to step off it, simply through the remembrance of your inherent worthiness, your truth as beings of love, yourself as a powerful creator, and stepping back into your sovereignty.

And so this is one way that the collective together is focused on the lower frequencies. But if all were to come together and focus on a shift to love, to healing, to restoration, regeneration, and collaboration, all focused together on the higher frequencies, this shifts the vibration of the planet. And you will see that which is feeding off of low frequencies loses its power, as there is no fuel left. You can shift the world. The key is to see all of the places where you are segregated into different groups, glamorizing being separate, or told that you are not one with another, and this is also how you become "separated" from yourself, as the One.

It is to step into integration that sets you free. It is to collaborate, to integrate, to be the One together, to harmonize together, that together you raise the heartbeat of your world. You allow the world to fully embody love. And it takes awareness, first, of the ways that you have been unconscious of this—to see the messaging, and where you are operating from automatic processing of separation consciousness. That being said, on a smaller scale, suppose you are focused on something on a micro-level. We can explore the dynamics of calling forward something with someone in your life, perhaps for your family as a unit.

The first thing to become aware of is differences in desires and frequencies between each—is everyone truly on the same page? Coming from the same frequency and calling in the same vibration, or is there dissonance? And so, this can power the manifestation, but if there are differences, you might notice that it doesn't come through in the way you want it to.

For example, what if two individuals were to clearly align themselves with the same job, and only one person can fill it? First it is to see that it all works out perfectly, and that that specific job is more about what they get from the job energetically than the job itself, and it is to be of a narrow mind to believe that only that one position can create this feeling or experience, and so whoever does not get the job (perhaps one, perhaps both), can be in the knowing that it was for the fruition of something greater. This is to exemplify how different beings, or groups of people, can call something in for them, but then, who does it go to? Quite simply, whoever is a stronger vibrational match for the thing, emitting a clearer signal, and when you are looking at groups of people, the number of people emitting a certain vibration will affect where the energy as a whole is pulled as well.

But it is to also see, if you are thinking of a "win/lose" situation, and perceiving it as only one person "wins," this is still rooted in the old way of being. Everything is being responded to perfectly through vibration, and so the person who perhaps "loses" on paper will still receive exactly what is meant for them, which could be something greater than expected—another opportunity, a lesson, and so on, and so it is not so simple as "winning" and "losing," but all are simply receiving what is in alignment with their vibration, their next opportunity for expansion, or an anchoring in of who they are, and such is the dance with the universe.

The pattern has been to categorize into good, better, best, worst, win, lose, and so on, and this is what keeps you in the illusion of right versus wrong, keeping yourself on the hamster wheel, and truly limiting your mindset to perceiving that there is only one way to get what is in your highest—what you have decided—and the key is to open yourself to something so much better. It is from the old way of thinking that you might find yourself in jealousy or anger, and this is one way you create these emotions for yourself, because you have already set yourself up for sadness or anger if you have decided to root yourself in the belief that only one can win and one can lose, compared to reframing what you think of as a "loss" as a win in itself. You might feel as though that seems too easy or unsatisfying, and it is your right to have those feelings. Here we remind you again that you can stay in whatever beliefs you like. We invite you to ask yourself, is this still serving you?

And so, if life is *flow* and life is happy, and you are a success every day, would you find this satisfying? For some of you, yes, and for others, in honesty, you might say no—if you are honest with where you are addicted to the emotional pulls, getting a hit of adrenaline from the intensity of the pain, or distracting yourself from creating and expanding *more*, by setting up beliefs so you stay in a cycle where you can never move past your current level. This is all up to you, but part of this process of truly stepping into your power is to realize all of the places inside where resistance or fear or doubt bubbles up, and you understand more and more that the only block has been you all along. It is a brave thing, a most loving thing, to be in that knowing. When you can see that the only person who can block you is you, you are limitless. And then you are able to face the one you are meant to face all along—yourself.

The truth is you have been facing yourself all along, through others, through the outside world, but it is time to look directly in the mirror, to see yourself, the truest version of yourself, and release the resistance. It all comes back to you. Seeing your power. Seeing your strength. Seeing yourself as love. Forgiving yourself. Loving yourself. Releasing the resistance to yourself. In full acceptance, you are in full love, and this is what sets you free.

We will affirm that through this you are receiving the codes, and you are remembering the codes—let yourself receive them. Where you are in resistance to these words—this is a helpful reflection point. And we wish to send you the truth that we send so much love your way, as you are unlocking what is meant for you—and coming home to yourself, your truth. And it is from here you can truly step into what you desire, create what you desire, and operate from the new way.

Are you brave enough to trust yourself? How interesting that this is not common in your world, but we feel the vibration of the planet shifting, and you would not be reading this text if you did not trust yourself, for your Soul guided you to these codes. There is a match for you here, and you will see how things begin to unlock. We invite you to simply let it happen, and to practice the new way through this. It is not to force or push, but to co-create. To ask every day—what is in alignment with my soul? And you will be guided. It might not make sense, but the intuition that speaks to you is taking you there, with a shortcut to receive exactly what you desire.

We will also remind you to consider—where are you not seeing what you already have right in front of you? It is interesting to always look forward, but the creator is not always looking forward, dreaming, but using that to feel into what she or he has in the now. In your life, you are love, you have love. You are joy, you have joy. It is to realize what is already here, and where is that not enough? As you start to notice where you are in the belief that there is not enough, you will notice where the energy of lack is coming from—and it is tricky, we will admit! But you are developing the awareness, and it becomes clearer and clearer along the way.

When you are wanting from a place of needing, of feeling that there is not enough of something—happiness, love, joy, success, abundance—it is with the foundational frequency of lack, and then what comes to you? But if you call in the same thing from finding it within yourself, and asking for an amplification or repetition, more of this, now you are in abundance, and you feel the ease at which what you desire flows to you.

part twenty-nine
Manifesting Money

We would like to discuss considerations for those of you who are looking to amplify energies in the most common places we sense requests—money, love, and personal skills.

Let us begin with money, and we will remind you to orient yourself from where you are in an energy of abundance, of more, of giving, of receiving, and where you are in an energy of not having enough. When you desire to call in more money, we will invite you to root yourself in your "why." Where does the desire come from? Get down to the root, deeper and deeper, being honest as you go.

For example, is it so you can invest in your business, buy more things for yourself, provide for your family? Have an easier life? (We will add that money may or may not help you achieve these things.) The key is to get to the energy from which you are manifesting—when from love, we have a solid foundation.

If you think of money as a physical manifestation of energy, it is key to realize where you are in the energy of abundance in your life, and where you are already "rich"—rich in love, family, creativity, and so on—and from this you can invite in more money—for abundance attracts in more abundance.

You can create an abundance of anything. The more you align yourself with the energy of "plenty and more" in all aspects of your life, you will feel your vibration shift. And with money, where is it going? How do you care for it? What does your current energy have to say about your relationship with receiving money itself? For many of you say you desire more, but it is not cared for or treated with love when it is received. When you encounter money and treat it with fear, worry, or resentment, these choices and energies send a signal to the universe that you are pushing away money, whether or not that is your intention, and so you will be supported in this.

Does your energy offer space for money? How will you care for it? Where is it going? What of the question—*if I am afraid of money, and I am vibrating in a fear state, then would I not attract more fear?* And so we will remind you what money is a representation of—it is a representation of abundance (although it might have other associations for you), and so your fear will attract more of that energy, which is not abundance per se.

And this is how it is interesting to see how it plays out for you to receive opportunities for money, for there are instances when in the low frequencies you might attract in "money" that is embedded with or attached to lower frequencies, and from there what comes of it? How else does this affect your life? Is this "dirty" money, money that doesn't stay, or is lost? There is much that can show up in your reality, but the process can simply be—*what is the energy I wish to call in, and how do I radiate that energy?* It is always within you—you are abundant if you allow yourself to see. And so if you want more of this, be in more of this, as you are, but it serves to be in awareness of how open you are.

Money is also representative of other energies—providing for you, giving you something to trade, and we will ask you to reflect on what else it represents for you. Here is the key to how open you are to receiving it—it is all in working with the energy rather than the physical thing itself. And where do you judge how abundance comes to you—in money or not? This is where you are anchored into your "why" again, because you might think you want more money, but what if we were to tell you that more money would end up creating more issues (this does not have to be your truth, but an example), and then would you still desire it? What if you never saw a physical manifestation of money but were always provided for, living comfortably, and felt love flowing in your whole life? These are the questions to start to think about.

It is to release the attachment to the physical object, for again, this is thinking too small, and to tune into the energy of what you would like to create, and open yourself to the many ways it could come through, and let your Soul guide the way to what is great. When you are feeling that you do not have "enough" in your life, you are vibrating with this energy, focusing on "not enough," and so what signal are you radiating out? Remember the universe wishes to work with you and will support your beliefs. What is it you believe to be true about one who receives money? What would be needed from you? What is it about your personality? You start to untangle all of the programs you might have, and recognize where you have been blocking yourself, and neutralize the energy so you can become rooted again in what really matters—returning to your truth as a being of love and abundance, and remembering that plenty, vastness, limitlessness is your truth, and when you are there, see what is provided for you!

part thirty

Manifesting Love

Let us speak on love for a moment—perhaps you are looking for a romantic partner. Again, we invite you to get rooted in your "why." How is it that you want to feel? What does it mean to you to have a romantic partner? When the root energy is feeling not good enough, or feeling incomplete, you see where the energy of lack is the foundational frequency, and how your vibration does not call in the partner you seek. It is true, as they say, that it all begins with your wholeness, which radiates out, and this is also how you build a strong relationship with another—to both be whole and to create more of this together, with a strong foundation to begin with!

And what if the "why" is from loneliness? Again, similar roots. What if you are truly aligned with your "why"—love, coming from a place of wholeness yourself? And so we ask you, are you available for love? What is it you believe to be true deep down about relationships—how that might shift you and your life, or what would change in your daily routine? Where is it that you are not connected to the love you already have in your life? When you have love all around you but don't fully *receive* it, again, this is sending a certain signal to the universe, and it will be responded to. Where you say "no thank you," the universe replies with something different.

It is to find the love in your life, the abundance in your life, and set the intention to have more of this. And within you, where are you energetically open, and feeling safe to fully be seen? Where are you in fear of the vulnerability, the openness? Notice this fear, and transmute it. Remember that love can come to you in many ways—notice where you might be judging how it might be coming to you—through whom, and in what way. And the key is in honoring what truly makes you feel the way you want to feel—staying clear on the energy of it, rather than the physical manifestation of the energy itself. This way you don't set limits on yourself.

For some of you, you might experience that great love through a romantic partner, for others not. The romantic partner might be how you expected, and perhaps the opposite. For some, you might experience that great love through your life's work, through collaboration, through your larger family, through giving back, through other relationships you didn't expect. Fill yourself with that love—there are no bounds!

part thirty-one

Mastering Your Craft

We will speak to personal skills—we are referring to when you desire to be better at a particular offering, to be the "best" at a certain thing, to become something that you perceive to be different than who you are. Our first point with this desire is, again, to recognize where this is coming from. Is it in feeling that you are not enough? That you do not have enough? We will offer that perhaps this is a place where you are in resistance to yourself. We remind you that the key is acceptance, full love for yourself. Instead of focusing on having a particular skill— what if you followed your natural inclinations and what you are already skilled at?

It is interesting how so many avoid what they are naturally good at, immediately judging it to be not good enough, but what you have a natural gift for is where you are designed to shine. And what satisfaction would it bring you to keep mastering this craft, and to step into something that feels natural for you, that feels effortless, and create beauty from this? When you are in an energy of judgment of yourself, where you are in resistance to yourself, you might find that you overlook your natural skills and abilities, and instead jump to what you believe will bring you the feeling you desire—admiration, love, respect, success. And it is here that you get on the hamster wheel again, and elongate the path to coming back to who you truly are.

For that is really what you seek—the love, the happiness, the success, the admiration—this comes from your wholeness, your love for yourself, from being in full acceptance, radiating your signal out so brightly that no one can miss your glow. The illusion is that it is from the thing itself, rather than how you do it, which is truly rooted in who you are. It is your unique gift. It is not that a musician or an artist or an accountant or a logger or a salesman or a farmer is better or worse, but it is their passion for what they do, their glow in how they do it, and you might notice that certain crafts or jobs seem more appealing simply when you come in contact with someone who has a knack for it, a glow about them, happiness from their skill. Is it truly that skill you desire, or is it the happiness, the abundance, the joy, the ease that you want to feel through it?

We will also offer that as you all start to follow your natural gifts rather than being in resistance, or fitting into a box of what you've been told is better than (sitting in illusion), you will notice how the world as a whole starts to fall into balance again, the frequency all around you shifts, and again, this is a reflection of yourself! You have been gifted with certain skills and desires for a reason, and you can spend time pretending to be someone else, but then you are missing the point of being the creator of your whole reality. It is an illusion to believe that you are meant to be someone other than who you truly are.

In these lessons, in these questions, in these messages, our aim is to invite you to come back to who you truly are. And many of you resist this because you want a clear answer—and so you jump to what feels tangible—*am I good at this or that? Should I be this or that?* And this is not exactly what we mean. We mean to invite you to notice how you want to feel, what you naturally enjoy—skills are not always tangible. When do you light up a room? When do you feel your best? How do you help people feel their best? When do you feel that your life is in flow? What are you genuinely excited to do every day?

You can sign up for a life of difficulty—that is your choice, but when you are at a frequency of difficulty, you are at a frequency of resistance, and you will see more difficulty and resistance in your reality. It is in this way that you will start to see that as you shift what you perceive to be one part of your life, your whole life shifts, because all is connected, it is all a reflection of you, different aspects of you, but you are whole.

Drop into the simple question of—*what do I want, from my soul?* Not ego. You will start to become aware that much of what you want might be what you have been told is what you want, rather than what your Soul is guiding you to. And the more you allow yourself to be with your own energy, you can start to learn your Soul again—the old friend that has always been listening to you, that is always with you, that perhaps you have turned the volume down on, but now you turn the volume up again, and you might be surprised what you discover! To uncover who you truly are can start with the simple choice of following your desire to sit on the grass rather than sit inside, to eat an orange instead of an apple, to wear a green shirt instead of a red one.

You see, it is in the simple moments of tuning into yourself that you start to uncover yourself. How do you really see, truly know, a loved one? Well, to think you know a "celebrity" is not the full picture—to know their habits, their deepest desires, and the simple things they enjoy is to more clearly see them. And so, can you see yourself in this way? Can you see yourself for the little things, for the full range of desires and experiences, to accept and love yourself through the fears and the doubts, anywhere you might have previously judged and forgotten the beauty of who you are?

It is all information to help you come back to yourself. And when you let your soul guide the way, you will see how clearly your physical reality aligns with your soul, and you have cohesion again between the external and the internal, and you are fully integrated as the One, of the One, with the One. When you see yourself in this way, you see others in this way, and without anything even physically changing, your perception is entirely different. And this is one way you manifest something different.

We will return back to the original point, for what if you are wishing to develop skills that are natural to you, that are in alignment with your soul, and wishing to become more and more? Again, it is the same offering—to be rooted in your "why," and ask yourself where you are judging that you are not already good enough. Where are you comparing yourself to another, and perceiving the comparison as them being "better" than you, rather than a display of how it is possible for you to be, and asking the universe to send this your way if and when it is in divine accordance with your soul, alongside focusing on its expansion. But the key is returning to your gift—what makes you uniquely you. It is your unique *how* that is your magic.

When you are in the knowing that you are whole, and perfect in your skills as they are meant to be now, and you continue to focus on the skill with love, compassion, and wholeness, you continue to expand the energy around it, with higher frequencies, and so it naturally grows and expands, and you effortlessly attract what will support its expansion to you— perhaps in the way of teachers, supplies, or drops of insight that allow you to step into the next level of mastery.

We will remind you—why would the next level be more important than the first? For the previous level is the foundation—it is of the utmost importance—and here we release the idea of what is better or worse, and accept all as the beauty of what is. As you continue to show up as the master of your craft, your action in alignment with this energy will allow the skill to become imprinted in your way of being, and you will see the mastery continue to expand more and more.

part thirty-two
Timing & Contrast

With this and the previous ideas offered, another piece we wish to remind you of is divine timing, and honoring the expression you chose in this body, within the constructs of time and space, and the experience of what you perceive to be moving "forward," allowing yourself to experience the progression with surprise, as if it's the first time, for this is an experience your Soul desired to have! And so, remember that what is for you, and what you are in alignment with, will be delivered exactly when and how it should. And when you are in a rush, this is where you are in resistance, where you are forcing, where you do not trust the higher aspects of yourself, your divine supporters, to bring things forward in the most miraculous way, and instead desire to let the lower aspects of yourself be in control.

What if this was in fact slowing things down? What if this was not allowing you to fully embrace the energy you desire?

What if forcing it into your *now* causes you heartache, despair, or more struggle? If this were to be the case, you would certainly learn a lesson from it, and this would not be a "bad" thing at all, but we offer to you another perspective. When you continue to ask from an energy of, "But where is it?! Why hasn't it yet come?" you see where you do not trust yourself, or the magnificence of it all, where you might still be in an energy of lack, where you are in impatience, where you are not enjoying the abundance of now.

You can always look to what you perceive to be the past and think, "I wish I had enjoyed my experience there more fully." Once you receive the thing, then what? It is already coming to you if it is for you, and so now your job is to celebrate, to be in happiness, to be in joy, and to enjoy the now, for when the next comes, there will be something else. Where are you in the habit of needing "something else" to focus on, and where is this distracting you from what is in your present?

For some, it's skipping over the abundance, the gratitude for what is right there, and for others, perhaps avoiding what you do not feel you are ready to look at. This is a belief, and we remind you that of course you are ready to look *exactly when you know*. This is when you are ready to expand— when you see what is not in alignment, this is where you feel the nonresonance, and you are conscious of where you are choosing to stay out of alignment with your soul, but it is clear to you the path forward—shifting into what is resonant, allowing yourself to be the fullest version of yourself.

And so we will ask you, who is to say that what you asked for is not already coming? Much impatience comes from lack of trust, and if you are not in the belief that it is coming, then consider if you are resonant with it coming to you now. If you are in full belief that you are the person, the energy, that is a match for the thing, there is no question. It is coming. There is no need for impatience. It is a time for joy in what is now, at this point in the journey, for every part is as beautiful as the next.

Where you feel your life passes you by is when you are always thinking in the future, but the now is all there truly is. So we ask you, can you allow yourself to receive your now? The more you receive your *now* to the fullest, imagine how that energy will magnify your next *now*, and all the *now*s in the future. Receive your *now*. It is the only perception that is truly real, and it is where you can soak in what you have created, and what is for you.

And so, we remind you of divine timing. There is no need to rush—what is there to rush for? If you are a vibrational match, you already have it, and if you already have it, if you already are it, then you can feel the energy in the *now*—there is no waiting required. From this, you receive more of it.

We will go a bit deeper here, for we feel this will illuminate more for some of you. How safe do you feel to radiate your energy out clearly and powerfully? Are you ready to see what you can create? This can call forward hesitations to your own power, to finally achieving what you've always said you wanted, to releasing old fears or patterns or relationships, to releasing old versions of yourself. Where does the old version of you feel like the safety net, a shell so that the world cannot see who you truly are? And beyond this, are you ready to see a true reflection of who you are?

For some of you might be afraid, we suspect unconsciously so, that if you are to stop dulling your signal, and ask for what you want, and see the results, perhaps you will not receive the results you want, and perhaps the reflection from your reality might indicate that you are "not good enough," not vibrating with love, and so on. This is important to address as this is where the deepest knot of the illusion lies, because it is from this place that you are still in judgment of yourself.

We wish to empower you with the remembrance of who you really are, and the remembrance that you get to choose to step into that energy any time you wish—you are love, you are radiant, you are abundant, you are whole, you are powerful, and you are the universe. And when you are fully emanating this knowing, when you are fully embodied with this knowing, then you realize the world is now yours. The fear is an illusion, and the reflection back is exactly what you need.

For to be love does not necessarily mean there are no challenges or hardships—these are the gifts that allow you to step into your next level of ascension in this incarnation, these are the opportunities to unlock the codes for your next level of mastery as a human, these are the initiations that allow you to know more of your soul, your abilities, to see and feel more of your love and compassion, for yourself and for others. This is the shift—to understand that all is perfectly designed for you, and to release judgment based on the illusion of what is "right" or "wrong."

We understand that this can bring up painful feelings for many who have gone through much hardship, and this is where we invite you to *be love* and allow yourself to feel the feelings—the sadness, the rage, the frustration, the misunderstanding. These are the experiences that bring you into a deeper state of questioning, and going back into questioning can be the thing that catapults you into higher awareness, broader perspective, and more opportunities.

Where have you been challenged with your belief in Source, in the creator, in God? How can pain be from love? This is to broaden your understanding even more deeply. Again, treat yourself with love, and allow yourself to feel your feelings. What if these experiences are meant to elicit exactly this—a questioning of your beliefs themselves, bringing you closer to your truth? For it is the deeper questioning that will align you with more clarity—either a shift in perspective or a broadening, but really a deeper connection to yourself, for it is *you* who will answer for yourself.

This brings us back to "knowing" versus *knowing*. You might be told something many, many times before you fully *know* in your body, and then you understand. This is when you feel the resonance in your soul, and you might not understand how or why, but you feel the energetic shift in your body. The experiences that bring us closer to ourselves are love. The experiences that allow us to fall deeper into gratitude, while it might be through contrast, are from love. The experiences that show us the depths of our strength, the depths of our love, the depths of our emotions—these are love.

It is experiencing this expression of your soul to the fullest—the rollercoaster might jolt you, but what was your experience at the end of the ride? What lessons did you learn? It is through these lessons, these experiences, that you create meaning. And is this not what so many of you seek, at your core? What is happiness without meaning? You might have happiness already within you, but miss it if you don't feel the meaning. And so, experiencing the range of your emotions allows you to feel it, to appreciate it, and to fully soak it in. For if you never had the sadness, would you experience elation to its fullest, or perceive everything to simply be neutral if it was all one frequency?

It is through the difference in frequency that we learn to perceive. What we enjoy, what we do not. What different colors are. What different sounds are. Without the difference in frequency, what would the human experience be? The different flavors provide richness, give the brain something to work with, allow you to tune into different ideas, and allow you to perceive the "moving forward" that you believe to be what gives this life meaning.

And again—what about the question for yourself—is "moving forward" what allows you to feel the meaning of life? These questions are meant to illuminate for you your own beliefs, and where you have limited your experience of happiness and joy in the now. This is building the skill of uncovering why certain things are not in your reality yet—because you perceive them to not be so (whether or not they are), because you have decided there are conditions to getting there, or because you're interested in a different frequency.

part thirty-three
Making Sense of Your Now

What we hope for you to understand about manifestation, while we have much to say, is that it is in fact a way to play with your universe, to dance with the world that you create. As this topic becomes more popular, we note that it is confused in conversations around "wanting"—and what really is a want?

The beauty of manifestation is understanding how the world is already working, how you are dancing with the universe, and what your Soul is teaching you, showing you, and offering to you. It is always occurring, and through this we hope you see how powerful you are, always—not just in certain moments. It is how you can find fun in life again, and also experience deeper meaning. It is how you can take back your freedom, your choice, and release feelings of being a victim to what is around you—there is a choice to be made, a lesson to move through, guidance (whether easy or difficult) into your next level of expansion.

But we ask you—what is the foundational frequency of the want? In a world where you are conditioned to always be in "wanting," (more from ego, than soul) it is no wonder that it might feel difficult to attract in what you desire effortlessly, because you are taught to come from an energy of "not enough," and then you receive more confirmation of "lack" energy in your life. What you learn through playing with manifestation is to start to play the game more consciously, not to start something you haven't been doing all along. You are experiencing a reality—you might as well understand how it works, and how you can flow with it, and create what you want from it and in it—deepen your experience with it.

In doing so, with understanding more of how manifestation works, the key is truly in uncovering more of yourself, something that so many avoid until later in life, if they explore it at all—but the energy of the world is shifting, and you feel the call. You know the call. There is no need to fear, because you are beauty. You are love. And so, the more you uncover more of yourself, the more you receive love. The more you uncover yourself as love, you radiate it out into the world, and the more you experience it. And at your core, this is what most of you truly want, deep down. Love. The illusion is when you believe it must come from outside—it is from inside that it comes externally.

And so, it all comes back to you, a beautiful expression of Source, of the One. And through this, you see the connection between all. You feel complete. You feel community. Yes, the feeling of community, community of love—it begins with you.

And so we ask you—what are you truly living for? This is how you create meaning in your life, all yourself. And where so many of you continue to run in circles is when you're chasing something, but unclear on what you're truly chasing, and so you are always left unsatisfied. What would satisfy you? What would fill you up? What feels "worth it," as you might say? When you become clear on what this is, what your goal is, you can identify the frequency, and many of you will be surprised to see that it is closer than you think. Again, it is all within you.

How do you measure your happiness? Bringing awareness to this aspect of yourself allows you to see where you set yourself up to bask in that happiness, to receive it, or where you might have already decided, unintentionally, that nothing will ever be enough. It is just as easy to say that nothing is ever enough as it is to say there is always more than enough—but it is up to you to choose your perspective.

When you identify what you are truly living for, you feel the frequency, and you attract more of it to you, and we will offer that for many of you, you might realize that it is soul alignment all along. It is resonance, it is love, because this is who you are. This is your truth. And when you live in your truth, when you are fully expressed in your truth, from love, you feel free. And is this not what you have been seeking all along? Where you have decided that specific material things allow you to feel this way might be where you have blocked yourself from receiving *now*. Where are you in the illusion that the physical will unlock the energetic shift? You take your power back when you realize it is the energetic shift, the feeling, the vibration, that unlocks the physical, and so the whole world makes sense when you turn things upside down.

Much of the popular rhetoric around manifestation that we see in your world has led some to the misunderstanding that it is connected to an energy of forcing, which, we offer, in many ways, might be missing the point of it all. When you unlock the codes of manifestation, you see that living in flow with the universe, stepping into your power, stepping into yourself and your truth—this is what allows what is for you to come to you, and is how you amplify your signal. But it is not an energy of forcing something to be yours, rather an energy of being the purest version of yourself, and thus receiving what is your match, receiving the opportunities that catapult you into expansion, and receiving aligned lessons along the way in this experience. Again we return to—it is all in your intention.

On the surface, it is to make a decision and become a vibrational match, but when the energy of the desire is working "against" the flow of the universe, and what is in your highest, now you find resistance to getting there. Where many get stuck in manifestation is becoming frustrated when they feel as though what they want is not coming their way. The larger lesson of this text is to allow you to understand that truly understanding these processes and utilizing them in their highest form is rooted in aligning with your soul and harmonizing with your soul, rather than resisting its tune and wishing it was another.

The key is in accepting and loving yourself— and you feel the harmony within yourself again.

Much of the discontent so many of you feel and label as a result of the external is simply the reflection of or avoidance of the discord within yourself. And the truth is, your Soul, your Higher Self, your divine guidance, your body are all communicating with you and looking to be in harmony, for this is how the universe flows. Frequencies that are like will harmonize together, and so through this process, we hope that you find comfort and beauty in your unique rhythm, for it is your unique rhythm, played clearly, beautifully, and powerfully, that will bring all those who are meant to listen straight to it!

Notice where your ego or aspects of yourself that are in resistance to your soul are trying to force things to their liking, which is really for their momentary comfort, rather than their greatest expansion, or harmony. The universe is always supporting you. It is to realize that signs from your body, issues with your job, difficulties in relationships and so on—while you might perceive them to be uncomfortable—are keys to unlocking your next level of mastery, powerful lessons that you are ready to learn, if you accept the lessons.

And in fact, an overall happiness comes when you do allow yourself to feel the intensity of the sadness or the anger, feel through it, flow through it, learn through it, integrate the energetic shift, and embody the lesson, recalibrating and harmonizing with your soul, raising the frequency of the music, and coming closer to yourself again through it all. Where you resist feeling it, where you stay stuck, is where you feel the chronic stress, chronic struggle, low-level nonresonance that leaves you feeling unsatisfied the whole way through. All areas of frustration are messages to you, showing you places to look for growth, leading you to the path that will give you what you truly seek—as you are not meant to stay "stuck" in a frequency that is not in alignment with your soul. You are not meant to feel endlessly stuck in what does not feel harmonious for you.

Your Soul speaks to you and through you, the universe speaks to you and through you, through others (truly other aspects of the One, of which you are a part), through your body, through synchronicities in your environment, and through the voice inside. And when we say the voice inside, it might be your own thoughts, it might be a feeling in your body, it might be dreams or images, it might be the inherent desire. Listening to your soul is the fast track to embodying truth, being in Love all the time, and yes—you were meant to live a life where you are always in Love! There is no need to question your deservingness of what you are made of and from. It is already within you, but it is up to you to see it.

And anything, anyone, anywhere that keeps up an illusion that you are not love, that you are not worthy—there is a signal from the Universe—this is not in resonance, for it pulls you away from your truth, and from here you find the way. There are messages all around, the question is—will you listen? We understand it takes courage and bravery, and these are already within you. You are surrounded by unseen energies that are always with you, always supporting you, here to lend courage if you forget for a moment that it is already within yourself.

But we will also invite you to explore—is it fear that you are feeling, or a deep knowing that the shift will change you? For it will! It will shift your frequency, your reality will shift, and thus you are onto the next lesson or experience. And so, much of it is the primal instinct to fear what you are not already aware of—the discomfort could be an attack according to this way of processing, and this is where you learn to transcend the primal instincts. This is not to say they do not serve you, but do they control you? Or are you ready to ascend into your next level of mastering this experience?

part thirty-four
Shifting Identity

We will say that right now is such a powerful time on the planet, as humans are making a shift, and where for so long the primal instincts and urges, and ego, have been leading the way—what has this led to? Much sickness, confusion, unhappiness, and discord among people. And now is the opening to where more are awakening to what it means to live in alignment with their soul, to come together with others through coming into harmony with themselves, to be in awareness of the many different signals they are receiving, and to practice discernment for themselves. This is freedom.

There is so much input coming your way, and many of you have become lost in it all and have not realized what is steering the ship. But as you build the muscle of awareness, becoming conscious of new perspectives, more possibilities, choice, and your own power, you are able to move beyond what is from fear, or automatic processing, be grateful for all of the potential input, and decide for yourself what is in harmony with your knowing, what is in harmony with your Highest Self, yourself as a sovereign being of love—this expression.

You will build the awareness of what is resonating with the version of you that has felt unsatisfied and stuck, and what you might have labeled before as nonresonant but is actually resonant with the version of yourself that you wish to become. The key is awareness, the key is gathering information, allowing yourself to view it all from compassion and love, and choosing for yourself what is in alignment.

And if you viewed your life this way—always taking care of yourself, choosing your beliefs and actions from true love for yourself and all others, in alignment with what harmonizes with that version of you (to which you are always connected), instead of what harmonizes to someone else, you will see that you are effortlessly guided to more of what allows you to feel the love of the world always with you. You will see that you are a powerful creator, and that the love, satisfaction, delight, happiness, joy, and peace do not come from the creation that is done, but rather *being* the creator of your life, being in the process itself, and thus you find happiness the whole way through.

It is through this exploration that you might find a shift in your perception of identity, and what that truly means, for this awareness calls into question your identity itself, and why so strongly you have held onto certain labels, or traits, and how they may or may not be the truth of who you are. The universe, the energies around you, respond to what you identify as, and it is what you identify as that typically represents the energies you are embodying. Where are you staying stuck for the sake of clinging to an identity, rather than allowing yourself to evolve and grow into other expressions of yourself? This is really evolving into more of yourself.

Many of you have been taught that the concept of identity is how you know yourself, but we encourage you to dive deeper—it is to see how identity can shift, and really to go even further into, *Why do I identify as I do? How might I use it to hide? And, in what ways am I putting myself in a box?* The key with identity is to release attachment—as you will see that your identity can change whenever and however you desire, for if it were fixed, how could you create something different? And watch yourself shift from fear of losing identity to releasing the need to have any single one—for the process of dancing with the universe is allowing yourself to be changeable, malleable, and unattached to any one thing, as you see that attachment to any one thing decides for you, based on your beliefs around it, what it means.

And so, we invite you to play with the idea of "identity" itself. Let yourself create your own meaning behind it—for it no longer controls you. As you build awareness, you are able to consciously shift your identity to who you want to be, the version of you who embodies that which you want to feel, and you can do this in a moment, and you can do it again, again, and again. It is when you truly identify as love, as joy, as peace, as who you wish to be, that you will see you have made the energetic shift that allows you to attract in more of that thing. And so, you can use identity as a tool, to your advantage.

Where has identity controlled you, or kept you stuck? Now, you can use this as a tool to attract in more of what your soul desires—when you identify as one who is worthy of and who embodies the frequency underneath that which you want, you will see it naturally flow through you, and to you. In this way you can work with the tool of identity, and you can also detach from it as a whole—liberating yourself to shift as you please.

part thirty-five
Surrender

We will return to the topic of surrender—another point of confusion in common language and messaging. We invite you to release any connotations you have attached to the term "surrender," for we understand that for some of you, the associations you have with the word might prevent you from being open to what this can unlock for you.

First we will point out that much of your world stays on the hamster wheel in an endless cycle of looking for "power," and that could be from a high or low frequency, because they think this will allow them to feel the frequency that will make them feel whole or complete. This in itself is missing the point of understanding what you are truly looking to feel. The reason why we point this out to you is because many of you believe you will find power in your lives by being in control, but there are many misunderstandings of how to be in control of your life, which is why so many feel helpless or victims to their circumstances. Our goal with all of this information is to empower you to have the tools to create positive shifts in your life, and for you to fully share your gifts and magic with this world. It is your right to experience joy, love, and fulfillment.

The misunderstandings are rooted in believing that if you try to gain control by forcing things, pushing or pulling things to be how you think you want them, then you will feel more in control. But many of you have the experience of this causing more things to spiral out of control, and you might end up living your life from an energy of always doing damage control, dealing with more problems, and so on. The reason why the result can come back to you in this way is rooted in the energy behind why you are attempting to control, which is often coming from dissatisfaction, frustration, and so on— not love.

And so we will bring the topic back to surrender, and hope this allows you to understand what we truly mean by this, because it is the frequency we wish to cover more than the words themselves. You may switch out the word to whatever suits you. What we mean by "surrender" is simply releasing resistance to what is in alignment with your soul, the true essence of *you* in your truth. What feels like releasing control for many of you is actually taking your power back, because in releasing the resistance, you allow yourself to flow with the universe, dance with it, and quickly reach how you want to truly feel, although it might not always make sense to you! This is to release resistance in the form of needing to understand logically how or why—the answer is that everything is energy, and when you feel the resistance, the block, energetically, through a low-frequency emotion, the energy of being "stuck," or feeling like you're getting nowhere, here is your message that you are not in harmony with your soul, and there is an easier way. This is where a single decision can shift and redirect the energy to align with harmony.

And so what you might call the "leap of faith" is truly just letting yourself float to what you are meant for, or rather, let it float to you (depending on your perception), and in working *with* the universe rather than against it, you in fact gain more "control" over your life, without all the trying, the pushing, or the pulling. The "surrender" is how you take your power back. The "surrender" is when you allow the highest aspects of you to create what is more magical and beautiful and expansive than you could have ever planned for. It is when you stop playing the game of illusions and start stepping into soul purpose— not as a destination, but as a way of living. You find yourself again. You find love again. You see how much is possible when you transmute, shift, and harmonize with energies rather than choosing to be in discord with them.

In allowing yourself to be the student of your soul, you become the master—at peace, one with yourself, one with the universe, being the One, and seeing the magnificence of it all, as an expression of you. And so, "surrender" is often the last piece, the piece that allows your next desire to come through to you, because it is the moment you stop pushing against the door to keep it shut, and simply let it fly wide open. This is your message to the universe, to the energies around you, that you are ready to receive the next piece of your journey, your next lesson, what you are calling in.

But when you are in resistance, when you avoid "surrender," when you let your ego make decisions over your heart, the signal is that the door is closed, and so you are not open to receiving. Surrender, in this context, is not giving up on yourself, but rather trusting yourself. It is releasing the resistance. It *is* "giving up" the old programs and limiting beliefs that have kept you out of your highest soul alignment. It is saying to your soul, *I am ready to be the most expansive version of myself, and I am ready to be in harmony with you. I am ready to play our tune loudly and clearly, and attract in that which is exactly for me.*

There is a deep knowing within that when you do surrender, you will see how the cards land—and here you can uncover any resistance to truth itself. Where you avoid truth is where you avoid yourself, and this is where you feel that constant, underlying humming of dissatisfaction, nonresonance—something is not quite right. Living in your truth, emitting your clearest, most powerful signal, requires facing truth. For if you are in illusions with yourself, you will see illusions all around you. You will find yourself trapped in illusions. When you face the truth of yourself, everything else will start to harmonize with you, and you will find yourself finally face to face with truth in your reality, a reflection of you being the highest vibrational version of yourself.

Many of you fear the dark because it represents the unknown. You wish to see things in the light, so you can see the truth. And so, why would this not be so when it comes to yourself? It is time to face your truth, your soul's deepest desires, the truth of your expression in this lifetime. It is from this truth you find acceptance, it is from acceptance you find yourself in love, and it is from being the truth of love that you are set free.

It is our hope that through this text you find yourself closer to yourself. Trust that through this text, codes have been unlocked deep within your cells to activate your knowing, and you will see your reality start to shift in alignment with facing this frequency, these words, and a new perspective, or perhaps a new way of seeing an old perspective. It is our hope that through this text you remember your own power, you remember that you are love, and that this is your truth. Where you feel lost, you understand that it is simply a signal that you are about to embark on a lovely journey of discovery, and that you are not "wrong" and you are not "bad" unless you decide yourself to be—but this is not how the world sees you.

All is energy. You are energy. We ask you to think about what your energy is, how you harmonize it, and what signal it is sending out. We hope that through this text you see there is an "easier" way—that you can master your reality through releasing much of the effort, and allowing yourself to be in flow with the universe. It is our hope that through this text you are able to unlock more of the magic that is always within the world, and more importantly, within you.

Remember that the universe is always supporting you and responding to your signals. It is time to remember the power you have in your life—and the way to this is simply through love. It is our hope that through these words you feel the frequency of love, joy, and freedom. *You* set yourself free. It is time to step into the highest version of yourself, for your soul has been waiting, and has always been ready. You are ready.

Be in love *now*, and see what you can create. Trust that your knowing is stronger than you think. It is time to let your truth guide the way. It is through this alignment that you shift the world, all through the shift in you. Watch as your internal process of expansion shifts everything around you. From this, you see what you are capable of. You see yourself as an extension of the One, a connection to all others. You see yourself as the One that is all, and all harmonizes once more into a beautiful chorus. We send you so much love.

From the Author

Channeling a book from a nonphysical entity was never on my radar. As a young girl, I dreamt of being an author when I grew up, but I imagined I would spend months at a time nestled in a cabin in the woods to work on fantasy novels. I forgot about that dream over the years as I focused on other career pursuits, but I somehow found my way back here in a way I never could have expected. Ironically, that's exactly what this book is about.

I had "tapped out" of my intuitive gifts for quite some time (or at least, tried to), until they started opening up again when I was in college, through the process of healing from multiple autoimmune diseases. One thing led to the next, and I went from spending my free time reading scientific journals on PubMed to energy healing and communicating with spirits.

It was my own health journey and entrepreneurial pursuits that led me to learning about manifestation. I was in such a dark place with my health that I was willing to try anything, so I began learning about energy work and the power of the mind. As I started incorporating these principles into my life, my body finally healed from chronic illness. Amazed at overcoming what many told me would be impossible, I started focusing on energetic alignment in every aspect of my life. Everything shifted.

Instead of feeling like I was dragging myself through life, everything started to flow. I saw signs every day. Opportunities kept dropping in my lap. I experienced a level of alignment and love in the relationships in my life that I had only dreamed about. My business was growing exponentially and flourishing while I did less work than ever before. It felt like I could easily create the things I truly wanted—simply with a shift in focus. Really, it felt like I could effortlessly *attract* the things I wanted—simply with a shift in focus. It was clearly not just coincidence, and it wasn't based on hard work. I couldn't believe how much my life had transformed, but really, I couldn't believe how much *my feelings* about my life had shifted.

I was no longer struggling with the anxiety or depression I dealt with my whole life, because I didn't feel powerless or purposeless anymore. I became one of those people who actually saw the glass half-full. (Those people used to really annoy me. I didn't think it was real.) Up until that point, I had spent my life always waiting for something to end or for something to come in order for me to finally be happy, or for things to get better. I no longer saw it this way—I saw every day as a miracle. Everything I wanted was in me. I was so happy with *being*.

As I progressed on my spiritual journey, I started infusing energy healing, neural reprogramming, and manifestation practices into my work with clients, and the shifts were profound. I witnessed clients heal seven years of chronic illness in just a few weeks. I saw clients go from debt to earning six figures in just a few months—some less. I witnessed people effortlessly call in their life partners, their ideal homes, and their dream jobs. Most importantly, I saw people become truly happy. Brighter. Authentic versions of themselves. They would tell me they felt free, and unstoppable.

We have so much more power than we know. My explorations of this concept only deepened when I started channeling. The messages that came through challenged me, expanded me, and made me see the world in a new way. It taught me a new level of discernment. Since sharing more of these messages with my community, I've seen how these messages do the same for others, inspiring them to step into who they really are.

MY EXPERIENCE CHANNELING THIS TEXT

I started receiving intuitive messages about channeling this book about a year and a half before doing so. I patiently waited, knowing it would come whenever my guides were ready. A few months prior, my spirit guides told me to set aside two weekends to write, one in April and one in May of that year—and so, that is exactly when I channeled this text. I spent a few hours each day over those two weekends letting the messages come through. In the end I only needed about three days (including breaks for nature walks), to channel this book. It felt effortless.

I didn't truly understand channeling until it started naturally coming through me. It was something I never expected to happen, but it is a beautiful gift that feels like pure love. The messages I have received have been incredibly helpful to me in my own life, offering me different lenses to look through that expand my mindset and allow me to find deeper happiness. That being said, I take every message simply as information that I get to think about for myself, not as inherent truth. My guides have told me that this is why clear information continues to come through—I stay neutral to it.

When I started communicating with the Monarch Being, I immediately recognized them as one of—if not the—most expansive, highest frequency entities I had worked with. I received messages from them for a few months, getting familiar with the vibration, before finally getting a "name." After expressing my frustration that they would only show me an "M" whenever I asked about a name, they finally called themselves the Monarch Being. Channeling them feels like pure love is pouring into my crown chakra, filling my entire body. The energy is distinct—a potent stream of divine feminine energy surrounded by divine masculine energy.

Their messages have truly expanded my consciousness and exposed me to new ways of experiencing my reality, rooted in love and understanding. That being said, the information they share is simply a perspective. My view on all channeled messages (really, all information—channeled or not) is to simply take it as a point of view and practice discernment for myself. I tune into the vibrational resonance, how it lands with different aspects of me, whether I find it helpful or not, and go from there. Again, it's not about giving your power away to anyone or anything else, but being open to another viewpoint, and seeing if you learn anything from it. Take it if it resonates, and leave it if it doesn't.

As I write this, the energy of the planet has shifted rapidly and intensely over the last few years, and it will continue to. This text is meant to aid us in our shift to a new way of being, and I personally found the information in this book to be incredibly helpful in explaining the many nuances of how energetic attraction works.

Quite a few of my own questions were addressed in this text, and I wouldn't be surprised if they're the same questions many others have as well. This text is truly meant for anyone who feels called to it, and it is laid out to explain manifestation from the basics to the more advanced nuances. Whether or not it all resonates with you, the Monarch Being has made it clear to me personally that the insights in this book will be core understandings to help our shift as a collective, navigating the new vibration of the planet.

Whether or not everything they say resonates with you, it truly is a transmission of love, and I hope you feel that energy transfer the way I did.

About Christina

Christina is an intuitive channel, celebrity energy healer, & founder of Ahai 7D Energy Healing. Her mission is to support individuals in stepping into their power, unlocking their intuitive gifts, and living their most authentic, abundant, and aligned lives.

After battling multiple chronic illnesses – and becoming a Functional Nutritional Therapy Practitioner to help herself and others heal through nutrition – Christina realized there was still a missing piece to her healing journey: spirituality. She was able to transform her life and build a 7-figure business by 25 through energy work, rewiring her brain, and manifestation. She then went on to download Ahai 7D – a powerful new form of energy healing.

Christina has helped thousands of people master the energetics of their businesses, relationships, and health through her membership, The Channel Collective, and transformational online programs. She is also the host of her own podcast, Christina the Channel, and founder of The Podcast Connector.

Visit https://christinathechannel.com/ to learn more.

CPSIA information can be obtained
at www.ICGtesting.com
Printed in the USA
BVHW030831280322
632626BV00012B/483/J

9 781957 048031